Jewish Education in *Transition*:

Proceedings of the First International Conference on Jewish Education

Edited by Zvi Grumet

THE LOOKSTEIN CENTER

Ben Yehuda Press
Teaneck, New Jersey

Published by Ben Yehuda Press
430 Kensington Road
Teaneck, NJ 07666

http://www.BenYehudaPress.com

ISBN 0-9769862-0-5
ISBN13 978-0-9769862-0-1
Library of Congress Control Number: 2006939560

1st edition
06 07 08 09 / 10 9 8 7 6 5 4 3 2 1

Other publications of The Lookstein Center

Jewish Educational Leadership (5 volumes)

Curriculum: Real teachers in focus
Oded E. Schremer and Stephen Bailey

To Study and to Teach: The methodology of Nechama Leibowitz
Shmuel Peerless

עיונים בחמש מגילות
גבריאל חיים כהן

Perspectives on Jewish Education

David the King
David Silber

Joseph and his Brothers: A story of change
Uriel Simon

The Community School: Proceeding of an online discussion
Zvi Grumet, ed.

Judaism and Modernity: Realigning the two worlds
Yitz Greenberg

THE LOOKSTEIN CENTER
for Jewish Education in the Diaspora
School of Education • Bar-Ilan University
+972.3.531.8199 +972.3.535.4980
Fax +972.3.535.1912
info@lookstein.org www.lookstein.org

Contents

Editor's Preface

Echoes of the educational imperative can already be found in the Torah's description of Avraham – that he instructs his children and his household to observe the ways of God to do justice and righteousness (Breishit 18:19). That theme is codified in the famous passage in the *Shema*, *veshinantam levanekha*, and has been on the lips of Jewish parents and children ever since.

But Jewish education has never been static. Originally the primary domain of the parents, the Talmud (Bava Batra 21a) records with ambivalence the transition from parent-centered teaching to community-based education, with R. Yehoshua ben Gamla's revolutionary institution of public education for all children. Later still, R. Ḥiyya (Ketubot 103b) launches his own initiative to ensure "that Torah not be forgotten from Israel." In every era since, each generation has sought ways to address its unique educational needs – the Babylonian yeshivot, the schools of Rashi and the Tosafists, community based *batei midrash*, the great Lithuanian yeshivot, the *gymnasia*, R. Samson Raphael Hirsch's *Torah Im Derekh Eretz*, the German Rabbinic seminaries, *Ḥassidic* yeshivot, Yeshiva University, the North American day school, the Israeli *Hesder* Yeshivot, the trans-denominational community school, Israeli post-high school programs for foreign students, Israeli pre-army *mekhinot*, Israeli secular Yeshivot, and the list goes on.

In January 2005, The Lookstein Center for Jewish Education of the School of Education at Bar-Ilan University and The Shul of Bal Harbour co-sponsored a conference on Jewish education entitled "Grounded in Tradition, Wrestling with the Present, Imagining the Future."[1] The focus of the conference was an initial exploration of the implications for Jewish education of our rapidly changing world. This engaging volume is one product of that conference.

The articles in this volume have been organized into two sections. The first addresses timeless issues which take on particular urgency

1 Partners included Yeshiva University's Azrieli Graduate School, The Center for the Advancement of Jewish Education at Florida International University, and Chabad of South Dade. Generous funding was provided by Targum Shlishi: An Aryeh and Raquel Rubin Foundation, and Citibank Surfside Financial Center.

in the modern world, essentially examining the transition between pre-modernity and modernity. Jacob J. Schacter opens the pages of history regarding the question of critical readings of the *Avot*; Stuart Zweiter challenges Jewish educators to critically look at themselves; Moshe Sokolow explores an educational agenda for the tension between universalism and particularism; David Pelcovitz brings us back to the ancient core of Jewish education, parenting.

The second section focuses on the transition between modernity and post-modernity, with the looming question of what is the stage beyond post-modernity. Scott Goldberg researches the impact of the exposure to media and Internet; David Schnall analyzes data from the monumental 2001 Jewish Population Survey; Yisrael Rich discusses research on identity development in teens; Irwin Mansdorf examines changing attitudes toward Israel amongst college-aged students in Israeli institutions; Elliot Malamet shares his own struggle with post-modern students; Mark Rosen looks at outreach programs in the post-modern era. Aryeh Rubin, whose Targum Shlishi foundation was a sponsor of the conference, dares the entire educational community to face the realities of a changing world.

It is our hope that this volume, like the conference, will continue to inspire thoughtful discussion leading to practice in the never-ending quest to educate and inspire the next generation of Jews.

Zvi Grumet
Jerusalem
Kislev 5767

I. From Pre-Modernity to Modernity

On the Morality of the Patriarchs: Must biblical heroes be perfect?

Jacob J. Schacter

On April 16, 1935, Rabbi Aharon Kotler, then head of the Etz Ḥayyim Yeshiva in Kletzk, Poland, published an article in Warsaw's *Der Judishe Togblatt*[1] defending the honor of the patriarchs and matriarchs which he claimed had recently been maligned in a series of articles entitled "*Ḥumash* Motifs" in the newspaper *Heint*. He wrote how shocked he was to see "the terrible blasphemies and the violation of the sanctity" of these great holy ancestors of the Jewish people printed there. He described his "shame" and "anguish" at this "betrayal," "travesty," "cynical ridicule," "insidious venom," "violation of the dignity of the patriarchs," and "defamation of the Creator, His Torah, and the holy patriarchs who form the very basis for the continued existence of the Jewish People." As a result, wrote Rabbi Kotler, he felt compelled to issue an uncharacteristic public statement protesting what he considered to be this rank disrespect. On the contrary, he wrote,

> The holy forefathers – who were the most luminous, loftiest, and purest personalities, the holiest creatures – represent the foundation of eternal spiritual vitality, the wellsprings of *ḥesed* and the full range of positive attributes, for the entire world, for all of mankind. The patriarchs are, in fact, held in the highest esteem by every nation on earth. The worst enemies of the Jews did not dare tamper with their luminous and holy image.

[1] The article is entitled, "Ofener Brief ful Kletzker Rosh Yeshiva HaGaon Rabi Aharon Kotler." I have used Rabbi Moshe Kolodny's translation printed in *The Jewish Observer* 24:2 (March 1991):50.

For a recent discussion of aspects of the biography and worldview of Rabbi Kotler, see Yoel Finkelman, "Ḥaredi Isolation in Changing Environments: A Case Study in Yeshiva Immigration," *Modern Judaism* 22:1 (February 2002):61-82.

Rabbi Kotler went on to insist that "every Jew possessing a spark of faith, to whom the honor of the Jewish People is dear, is forbidden to allow such heretical writings . . . to enter his home" and appealed to "rabbis, *gaonim*, *talmidei ḥakhamim*, as well as to ordinary God-fearing Jews to protest this sacrilege as strongly as possible."

What aroused the ire of Rabbi Kotler was a series of poems by Itzik Manger, Yiddish poet, playwright, parodist and literary essayist. Successive Friday issues of *Heint* had featured Manger's poetry on a variety of biblical themes from the Book of Genesis entitled, for example, "Hagar's Last Night by Abraham," "Hagar Leaves Abraham's House," "Abraham our Father Scolds Lot," and "Lot's Daughters."[2] I cite one in translation, "Hagar Leaves Abraham's House," as an example of what precipitated Rabbi Kotler's protest:

The dawn is blue at the window,
Three times the rooster crowed.
Outside the horse is neighing,
Impatient for the road.

Hagar is worn with weeping,
Her child lies in her arms.
Once more she casts her eyes around
The gray familiar room.

Outside the wagon-driver haggles
With Abraham for his fare
"R. Avraham, add a six-piece,
After all, there are two to haul."

The pony scrapes the gravel
As if it were saying, "Come on!
Give me a chance to show you
How to make the highway tame."

---

[2] The first two were published in the March 29, 1935 issue and the next two the following Friday, April 5, 1935. They were reprinted, with some changes, in Itzik Manger, *Medrish Itzik* (Jerusalem, 1984), 17-20, 29-32. My thanks to Rabbi Dr. Shalom Z. Berger and Shulamit Z. Berger for bringing these sources to my attention and making them available to me.

"Cry not, dear Yishmael,
Our portion is like this.
This is how the patriarchs behave
With their long pious beards. . . "
(*Ut azoi firen zikh di avos*
Mit di lange frume berd.)

There he stands wearing a silken cap
Rav Avraham the pious Jew.
"Loyal mother, does he at least feel
My bitter broken pain?" . . .

And Hagar takes as a witness
The heaven and the earth.
This is how the patriarchs behave
With their long pious beards.[3]

Manger himself acknowledged the irreverent nature of these poems at the beginning of his introduction to the work where they, as well as others similar to them, were published. "The poems gathered in this book are a sort of mischievous toying with the gray beards of the patriarchs and the head-shawl corners of the matriarchs," he wrote.[4] He concluded the introduction in a somewhat similar vein with the following prayer:

> I praise Thee Lord in Heaven, I praise/ Thee God for strengthening my days./ I thank Thee that with hand so weak/ I've finished just the same this work./ Diligence and care I've taken/ And the patriarchs I've wakened/ From holy texts and silver dust/ That hardened on them like a crust./ Here they stand, prepared to give/ You proof that they are now alive;/ To greet, dear readers, each of you/ With a cheerful, "Howdy-

[3] This translation, with some changes, comes from Leonard Wolf, *The World According to Itzik: Poetry and Prose* (New Haven and London, 2002), 13-15.

[4] *The World According to Itzik*, p. 3.

> do?"/ They with their holy mouths will tell/ Of many wonders, all so still.[5]

Of course, a full appreciation of Rabbi Kotler's response is only possible knowing the kind of language generally used in the Eastern Europe of the 1930s to describe the *avot*; it can only be assessed within the specific context of its time and place. However, measured against some contemporary expressions, Manger's formulations would qualify as veritable paragons of piety.[6]

Rabbi Kotler returned to this theme at least once after arriving in the United States in 1941, focusing on it in an address to a group of Jewish educators in the Fall of 1960. Notes of the lecture by one of the attendees were published shortly after they were delivered[7] and again eight years later.[8] Their status as an authoritative rendition of Rabbi Kotler's position on the matter was confirmed by their inclusion in the third volume of the collected works of Rabbi Kotler published by his closest students.[9] Here too, in the context of discussing the conflict between Sarah and Hagar over Isaac and Ishmael, he reiterated and underscored his notion of the absolute perfection of the patriarchs. He maintained that it is "absolute heresy" (*kefirah mamash*) to apply "the conceptions and world view of regular people" to these figures. He denied that the patriarchs had any imperfection (*pegam*), even "the slightest of the slight (*pegam dak min ha-dak*)," and refused to consider the possibility that they may have been "influenced by subjective ten-

---

[5] *Ibid.*, p. 5.

[6] For examples of disrespectful language about the *avot* written in the last decade or so, see Burton L. Visotzky, *The Genesis of Ethics* (New York, 1996), 31-32 and throughout the book and Naomi H. Rosenblatt and Joshua Horowitz, *Wrestling with Angels* (New York, 1995).

[7] R. Eliyahu M. Bloch, *Yalkut Midah Keneged Midah* (Lakewood, 1962).

[8] See "Ha-Derekh ne-Nekhonah be-Hora'at ha-Tanakh," *Shema'atin* 15 (Kislev 5728):8-13.

[9] See R. Aharon Kotler, *Mishnat Rabi Aharon* 3 (Lakewood, 5748), 177-87. For an English translation, see Yehoshua Leiman, *The Best of Light Magazine* (New York, 1995), 17-36; repr. in Rav Aharon Kotler, *How to Teach Torah* (New York, 2000).

dencies and desires (*mushpa'im mi-netiyot u-me-rezonot atzmiyim*)."[10] And, in fact, this "perfection model" of the patriarchs was expressed by others as well, either in programmatic statements about the role of the patriarchs in Jewish tradition[11] or as an exegetical methodology in commentaries on the Torah.[12]

An alternative view to that of Rabbi Kotler was promulgated by Rabbi Samson Raphael Hirsch in a number of different places in his commentary on the Torah. In one place, his point of departure is the well-known statement of Naḥmanides (on Genesis 12:10) that "Abraham sinned a great sin, albeit unintentionally," when he sent Sarah to the household of Pharaoh after having come down to Egypt because of the famine that struck the Land of Israel. This comment afforded Rabbi Hirsch an opportunity to reflect in general on the issue of the proper approach one should take to the patriarchs.

> The Torah never presents our great men as being perfect, it deifies no man, says of none, "here you have the ideal, in this man the Divine became human." . . . The Torah is no "collection of the examples of saints." It relates what occurred, not because it was exemplary but because it did occur. The Torah never hides from us the faults, errors and weaknesses of our great men. . . . It may never be our task to whitewash the spiritual and moral heroes of our past, to appear as apologists for them. They do not require our apologies, nor do such attempts become them. Truth is the seal of our

---

10 *Shema'atin*, p. 10; *Mishnat Rabi Aharon*, pp. 179-80. This article provoked an exchange in subsequent issues of *Shema'atin*. See *Shema'atin* 16 (Adar-Iyyar 5728):86-87; 17 (Sivan-Av 5728):5-8.

11 See, for example, R. Eliyahu Eliezer Dessler, *Sefer Mikhtav me-Eliyahu* 1 (Jerusalem, 1959), 161-66; 2 (Bnei Berak, 1964), 160. See too R. Ḥayyim Eizik Sher, *Avraham Avinu: Hitboninut be-Ma'asei Avot* (Jerusalem, 1946); R. Hayyim David Halevi, *Aseh Lekha Rav* 5 (Tel Aviv, 1983), 400-01, #115. While there are differences between these sources, they share the basic "perfection" model. See also Eliezer Margaliyot, *Ha-Ḥayavim be-Mikra ve-Zaka'im be-Talmud u-ve-Midrashim* (London, 1949).

12 See, for example, Amos Frisch, "R. Jacob Zvi Meklenburg's Method in the Issue of the Patriarchs' Sins," *Journal of Jewish Studies* 53:1 (Spring 2002):107-19.

> Torah, and truthfulness is the principle of all its true and great commentators and teachers.

Rabbi Hirsch added that not only does such a view not detract from the greatness of the patriarchs or other biblical heroes but, on the contrary, it enhances it. "If they stood before us as the purest models of perfection, we should attribute them as having a different nature, which has been denied to us. Were they without passion, without internal struggles, their virtues would seem to us the outcome of some higher nature, hardly a merit and certainly no model that we could hope to emulate." For example, continued Rabbi Hirsch, the great humility the Torah ascribes to Moses (Numbers 12:3) can only be fully appreciated by knowing that, on occasion, he could lose his temper (Numbers 20:10).

It would appear, then, that Rabbi Hirsch takes a very different approach to that of Rabbi Kotler. Not only, in his view, do the patriarchs have "faults, errors and weaknesses," but the Torah does not hesitate at all from presenting them in all their details.[13]

In my public presentation I noted that the first step for Jewish educators who teach *Ḥumash* is to appreciate this issue *per se*, to understand and be sensitive to the multiplicity of opinions on the question of the "perfection" or "humanity" of the patriarchs, or other biblical heroes for that matter, from the rabbinic period up to contemporary times. There is a large and growing literature on this subject, drawing on a wide variety of theological, exegetical and polemical texts.[14] But

---

13 R. Samson Raphael Hirsch, *The Pentateuch, Vol. 1 Genesis* (New York, 1971), 236-37 (on Genesis 12:10). See also Rabbi Hirsch's comments on Genesis 25:27 (p. 425): "Our sages, who never objected to draw attention to the small and great mistakes and weaknesses in the history of our great forefathers, and thereby make them just the more instructive for us ...;" *The Pentateuch, Vol. 2 Exodus* (New York, 1971), 73 (on Exodus 6:14), regarding Moses' "perfectly ordinary human nature, subject to all failings and weaknesses, to all the limits and requirements of human beings, just like all other men amongst whim he had been born and grown up . . ."

For a discussion of Rabbi Hirsch's position, see Joel B. Wolowelsky, "Kibbud Av and Kibbud Avot: Moral Education and Patriarchal Critiques," *Tradition* 33:4 (1999):35-44.

14 Much has been written, for example, on the Talmudic statement (*Shabbat* 55b-56b) that "Whoever says that David (and others) sinned, can

after having mastered the literature on this issue, and having come to his or her own personal conclusion, the educator must then very carefully examine how potentially "problematic" biblical stories that present biblical figures in a less than perfect light should be taught to elementary and high-school students. It is one thing to arrive at one's own conclusion on this issue; it may be something else to determine how to present those conclusions in class where clearly, for example, grade level must be a major consideration; what is appropriate in eleventh grade is surely not appropriate in fourth grade. If, as I would suggest, the ultimate goal of a yeshiva education is to produce young men and women who love Judaism and are inspired to maintain a life-long commitment to our *masorah*, or Jewish tradition, then great thought must be given to how to present apparent patriarchal imperfections to students.

And, in fact, both the Rabbi Kotler model and the Rabbi Hirsch model pose conceptual challenges. First, how does Rabbi Kotler account for the many rabbinic and medieval statements with which he was undoubtedly familiar that seem to explicitly assert patriarchal misbehavior? Indeed, rabbinic literature is full of statements like that of Naḥmanides just cited, and some even more sharply formulated. The Talmud considers the Jewish people's forced enslavement in Egypt as a punishment for Abraham having committed one of three

only be mistaken."

A number of relatively recent publications on this general subject have generated heated debate: R. Shlomo Aviner's article, "Tanakh be-Govah Eynayim" elicited much reaction in the newspaper *Ha-Tzofeh* from April-June, 2002 (http://www.hazofe.co.il/web/mador.asp?Modul=24&kod=132&kod_gilon=499); R. Yuval Sherlo's article, "'Asher Banu Shtehen et Bet Yisrael'," in Ofir Schwartzbaum and Amichai Sadan, eds., *Ketonet Or* (Jerusalem, 2000), 413-22 and R. Tzvi Yisrael Tau's book, *Tzaddik Be-Emunato Yiḥyeh*. For the polemical context, see David Berger, "On the Morality of the Patriarchs in Jewish Polemic and Exegesis," in Clemens Thoma and Michael Wyschogrod, eds., *Understanding Scripture: Explorations of Jewish and Christian Traditions of Interpretation* (New York, 1987), 49-62; repr. in Sholom Carmy, ed., *Modern Scholarship in the Study of Torah* (Northvale, 1996), 131-46; Ofir Mintz-Manor, "Mah Atah Noten Pitḥon Peh le-Minim?: Le-Pitronah shel She'elat ha-Ẓenzurah be-Piyutim le-Shavuot," *Tarbiẓ* 70:3-4 (2001):637-44.

potential wrongdoings.[15] Radak harshly criticizes Sarah for the way she treated Hagar and claims that the Torah included the story about their disagreement as an example of how *not* to behave.[16] And there are many more such examples. I am beginning to develop a carefully nuanced understanding and appreciation of Rabbi Kotler's position that would explain it even given these apparently contradictory statements, but it is beyond the scope of this brief paper. Second, how does Rabbi Kotler respond to the "didactic argument" of Rabbi Hirsch? If, in fact, the patriarchs are perfect, of what pedagogic purpose is the Torah's description of their behavior? How can any individual be inspired to emulate them if their fundamental makeup is so unlike that of anyone else? Both of these issues will undoubtedly be raised by thoughtful students and need to be addressed.

Teaching Rabbi Kotler's position poses one final challenge that is not a criticism of him but rather of contemporary culture which has been deeply embedded in parts of the Modern Orthodox community as well. Writing in 1835, Alexis de Tocqueville already noted the "general equality of condition" he discovered in the United States which, he suggested, kept its citizens from acknowledging the greatness or superiority of any single idea or even any particular individual. Because America is a democracy, he asserted, all of its citizens are considered to have been created equal, none greater or on a higher level than anyone else.[17] George Orwell began his review of Gandhi's autobiography by asserting that "saints should always be judged guilty until they are proved innocent."[18] The status of sainthood is never simply bestowed; on the contrary, the operative assumption is that it is inappropriate and undeserved. In contemporary America where the personal behavior of a president of the United States was shown to be utterly inappropriate and embarrassing, our students quickly develop a huge degree of cynicism about the greatness of any authority figure.

---

[15] *Nedarim* 32a. For other rabbinic texts that take Abraham to task for saying to God, "How do I know that I will inherit it?" (Genesis 15:8), see *Midrash Tanḥuma*, Parshat Vayigash 2; *Midrash Shir ha-Shirim Rabbah* 1:4.

[16] Radak, Commentary on Genesis 16:4.

[17] Alexis de Tocqueville, *Democracy in America* (New York, 1966).

[18] George Orwell, "Reflections on Gandhi," in *In Front of Your Nose, 1945-1950: The Collected Essays, Journalism and Letters of George Orwell* 4 (New York, 1968), 463.

And so, in a culture where we shrink everyone to Lilliputian dimensions, how hard it is to expose our students to the fact that there were people who lived who had no imperfections whatsoever, even "the slightest of the slight."

But, while Rabbi Hirsch's position is closer to and resonates more fully with the assumptions of our culture, it too poses a significant challenge for it opens up the proverbial Pandora's box. Is it now appropriate to ascribe whatever "faults, errors and weaknesses" we want to the patriarchs? Is there a line to be drawn beyond which such ascriptions are inappropriate?[19] Where do we draw the line? Can they, in fact, be considered just like you or me? Do we not refer to God repeatedly in our daily prayers as "the God of Abraham, the God of Isaac and the God of Jacob?" Do we not conclude the first blessing of the *Amidah* by referring to Him as "the shield of Abraham?" Clearly we assert, and to my mind must genuinely believe, that they are just not like "you and me;" indeed, they are much, much greater, an entirely different dimension of being. In the words of Gary Kamiya, "To feel the pedestal is to call the very idea of the pedestal into question."[20]

It is incumbent upon *Tanakh* educators squarely to face this issue and construct an approach that will resonate, first for themselves and then for their students, whatever age they may be.[21]

---

19 See the books cited above, n. 6.

20 Gary Kamiya, "Falling Out with Superman," *The New York Times Book Review* (January 23, 2000), 35.

21 For various approaches to this issue, see Yitzchok Adlerstein, "On Football: The Avot and Recent Disputes in Israel," *Jewish Action* 50:2 (Spring 1990):33-36; Hayyim Angel, "Learning Faith From the Text, or Text from Faith: The Challenges of Teaching (and Learning) the Avraham Narratives and Commentary," in Jeffrey Saks and Susan Handelman, eds., *Wisdom From All My Teachers: Challenges and Initiatives in Contemporary Torah Education* (Jerusalem and New York, 2003), 192-212; Avishai David, "Perspectives on the Avot and Imahot," *Ten Da'at* 5:2 (1991):24-26; Howard Deitcher, "The Child's Understanding of the Biblical Personality," *Studies in Jewish Education* 5 (1990):167-82; *idem.*, "Between Angels and Mere Mortals: Nechama Leibowitz's Approach to the Study of Biblical Characters," *Journal of Jewish Education* 66:1-2 (2000):8-22; trans. with some changes in *Iyunim be-Ḥinukh Yehudi* 9 (2004):193-211; Zvi Grumet, "Another Perspective on the Avot and Imahot," *Ten Da'at* 6:1 (1992):25-27; Emily Shapiro, "Approaching the Avot," www.atid.org.

From the Inside Looking in: Some musings on day school education

Stuart Zweiter

Honest reflection

Aristotle's observation about education – "this is not a question about which thoughtful people easily agree" – is as relevant for us today as it was for him. No single formula, vision or model works for everyone, but engagement with different perspectives enriches us and brings us closer to some form of a better understanding or at least a better approach.

My purpose here is to encourage serious reflection, to suggest a framework in which we can take a good look at ourselves and each other in a spirit of genuine openness, both individually and collectively. To borrow from Cassius' reply to Brutus:

> Therefore, good Brutus, be prepared to hear
> And since you know you cannot see yourself
> So well as by reflection, I, your glass,
> Will modestly discover to yourself
> That of yourself which yet you know not of[1]

Were we as Jewish educators or lay people associated with a particular school, or for that matter as a community, to ask, "mirror, mirror on the wall who is the fairest one of all," we should be very concerned about the kind of reply we would receive about the state of Jewish education from an honest mirror.

Maimonides[2] identifies four sources of intellectual error, three of which are already suggested in the writings of Alexander of Aphrodisias. The fourth, which is his addition, he refers to as habit and education. People, Maimonides says, naturally love the things to which they are accustomed, including opinions. For this reason, he says, many people fail to perceive the truth and cling to errors. His main area of concern is truth in spiritual matters, but it applies to and

1 Julius Caesar, Act 1, Sc. 2.
2 The Guide to the Perplexed I:31

is detrimental in all areas of intellectual endeavor as well. Intellectual honesty demands that each of us internalize the notion that there are other ways – often better ways to do the things that we do, and it is important that we be open to them. Certainly the best professional is one who is always learning, who is always open to new ideas, who is never arriving but always being on the way. In Jewish tradition, the term for a great scholar is *talmid hakham*, literally translated as "student of a wise man" or "wise student," expressing the notion that even the most outstanding scholar remains always a learner, a student.

Two anecdotes

Robert Coles, the wonderful Harvard professor of psychiatry and medical humanities, in his book "The Call of Stories," discusses and demonstrates how the power of stories enhances our understanding of ourselves and others, our values, our past and our future, and of issues in general. I would like to suggest a framework for our discussion using two anecdotes, ones which paint in full color, the potential and intensity that we need to strive for in Jewish education.

Shortly after the march from Selma to Montgomery, Abraham Joshua Heschel wrote to Martin Luther King:

> The day we marched together out of Selma was a day of sanctification. That day I hope will never be past to me – that day will continue to be this day. A great Hasidic sage compares the service of God to a battle being waged in war. An army consists of infantry, artillery, and cavalry. In critical moments cavalry and artillery may step aside from the battle-front. Infantry, however, carries the brunt. I am glad to belong to infantry! May I add that I have rarely in my life been privileged to hear a sermon as glorious as the one you delivered at the service in Selma prior to the march.

For Heschel, the march had spiritual significance. He wrote,

> For many of us the march from Selma to Montgomery was both protest and prayer. Legs are not lips, and walking is not kneeling. And yet our legs uttered

> songs. Even without words, our march was worship. I felt my legs were praying.[3]

The second story is about a particularly successful and intelligent businessman whose secular education included a B.Sc. from M.I.T. and an M.B.A. magna cum laude from Harvard Business School. He writes:

> Growing up I was unusually devout and passionate about God and Judaism, although the suburban community context I was in did not really support a life of piety, faith and prayer.
>
> In my senior year of high school I met a very charismatic "mystic" Hasidic Rabbi (Shlomo Carlebach) who used to go around the country giving "concerts" which were really prayer meetings over which he would preside, playing guitar and leading Hasidic worship songs, interspersed with religious story-telling and teaching. He had a large following among Jewish hippies and college students. I fell in with him, and spent the following summer traveling with him in Israel in his entourage.
>
> I wanted to live my life for God and with God, and while in Israel I considered abandoning my plans to go to M.I.T. in order to stay in Israel studying at one of the Jerusalem yeshivas (which are schools where young men devote their time to prayer and religious study, the closest thing Judaism has to religious life).

---

[3] Susannah Heschel, "Theological Affinities in the Writings of Abraham Joshua Heschel and Martin Luther King, Jr.," in *Black Zion: African-American Religious Encounters with Judaism*, ed. Yvonne Chireau and Nathaniel Deutsch (New York: Oxford University Press) and *Conservative Judaism* vol. 50, no. 2–3 (Winter/Spring 1998).

> But I was turned off by a certain sterility and coldness which I saw in them, and which did not speak of real intimacy with God.[4]

This man eventually converted to Catholicism.

I believe these two stories will help provide us with richer frames of reference in which we can more imaginatively and dramatically reflect on the questions raised in this paper.

For whom is education designed?

Perhaps the most fundamental kinds of questions that need to be asked are: What is our aim in religious education? In Jewish studies? How do we make the decision regarding what is the most appropriate educational program? What kind of education speaks to students most effectively and provides an adequate base for living a rich Jewish life?

I would like to first examine these questions from the perspective of education and schools generally, and then particularize the discussion to the issue of Jewish schools.

Permit me to begin with the observation that studies and statistics suggest that there is today declining literacy, decline in the general competence of young people, and increasing violence growing out of the failure that is contemporary education. This is true both in the United States and in Israel.

In so many discussions in the world of general education about how best to teach children, we don't often hear about the purpose of education other than as a social obligation and the preparation of the child for the adult world (work, career, etc.). Even a cursory observation of the reality in most schools will verify that discussions focusing on educating the intellectual, emotional, physical and spiritual elements of the child remain essentially in the realm of discussions, and are most often not realized in school programs.

How many educators really bother or manage to step out of theory into the lives of children to really explore what learning is for children? What really energizes and directs what schools and educators

[4] Roy Schoeman, "Unsought and Undeserved", *The Hebrew Catholic*, (78) Winter-Spring 2003, pp. 9-12.

decide to do in their educational programs? How many schools really work on creating educational environments for students that are academically appropriate, culturally sensitive, and compassionately caring? And how often can we honestly say that we are successful in that?

I suspect that many of our school practices are geared more toward helping teachers and administrators run their educational facilities efficiently than designed to provide healthy educational environments.

Take, for example, the practice of lining up. Does that serve a significant developmental need for the student? Or homogenous grouping – while it may be easier for the teacher to teach students who are at a similar ability level, it is far from clear that bright children learn less when they are with a mixed group of students than when they are with other bright children. Or tests and grades – do they provide valuable educational feedback for parents and students or are they simply an efficient bureaucratic method of accountability? And for each of the examples cited, what are the negative effects they have on the students?

Arthur Foshay, the great educator from Teachers College at Columbia University, emphasized that if a student cannot give a good answer to the question of why he is studying what he is studying, he probably should not be studying it. Do schools mostly end up nurturing and encouraging a system that subtly, and perhaps not so subtly communicates to the student that it is not the actual learning that is valuable but rather the achievement?

Defining better education

What is the child's perspective in the learning process? Why should he really care about most of the subjects that he or she learns in school? Most subjects are so abstracted and distant from a child's life and interests that it would seem odd if the interest were there. Children are naturally curious, but I would think that their understanding of what it means to learn has nothing to do with absorbing a particular body of knowledge. Learning is the consequence of exploration driven by curiosity. Information is collected, not as a commodity in itself, but as an adjunct to the process. Information is a tool that helps drive further exploration. No matter how logical doing something may be in the eyes of educators, it does not seem particularly productive if students are alienated from the process. If the educational process is turning students off, is it really educational? I believe that we have better options.

Progressive educators such as Dewey, Kilpatrick, Goodlad, Sizer, Paul Goodman, Neil Postman and Steven Harrison would claim that a school is good when it values questioning, problem solving and research, and deemphasizes memorization and ventriloquizing. Active student involvement, independence, critical thinking and questioning need to replace passive learning. Many students are programmed to succeed as students – they perform magnificently on standardized tests but may remain unable to think creatively. As Daniel Goleman has eminently demonstrated, cognitive intelligence is less a predictor of life success than emotional intelligence. Having the students understand their own feelings is an important part of their growth and can contribute much to their ability to learn; academic success is enhanced in environments that nourish the character and the self-awareness.

Research indicates that active learning helps develop critical thinking and enables the learning to be absorbed meaningfully. Learning experiences that engage the senses, emotions, and imagination alongside the intellect are more likely to have a lasting impact, and faculty can be the guides to student exploration. Alfred North Whitehead, the great 19th and 20th century mathematician and philosopher, maintained that "your learning is useless to you till you have lost your textbooks, burnt your lecture notes, and forgotten the minutiae which you learn by heart for the examination."

Schools need to adjust their programs to reflect the understanding that their primary responsibility is to the overall development of their students. While schools cannot ignore the requirements of high schools and universities, they should not act solely as preparatory and processing agencies for those institutions of higher learning, but as vehicles for fostering healthier and more productive individuals and a healthier society.

Steven Harrison writes,

> the child becomes a proxy for the parent's own unfulfilled dreams. The earlier these dreams are realized the better. Even babies should be learning. The

> Mozart effect in the crib, Baby Einstein videos when they awake... all part of the parent's drive to perfection. The pressure to achieve, the competition for resources. The fear that my child won't make it, that I won't make it.[5]

A pressured babyhood becomes an overscheduled, overachieving, and pressurized childhood. Is it any surprise that children are blowing up, breaking down, tuning out, withdrawing, measuring their worth by their test scores and designer jeans and communicating through pagers, cell phones, and instant messaging in order to hook up for drive-by relationships, drive-through food and driven lives?

They are simply displaying the education they received at school and home – to be faster and better, or more precisely, that they were not fast enough or good enough. Some learned to run harder, some learned to give up.

A few exceptions, endowed with an unusual measure of common sense and innate trust in themselves, learned that they are just fine as they are, whatever they are. These few children were lucky to be slow learners, that is, they never learned the way they were "supposed" to learn, just the way they naturally learned.

The role of tests needs to be similarly re-examined. Regarding standardized tests, Neil Postman has written that the curriculum often degenerates into coaching for the test. In some cases this would no doubt represent an improvement, but let us remember that the makers of standardized tests are businesspeople with their own agendas, the least of which being the best interest of individual children. The same concerns hold for testing done by individual teachers. The standard student question about whether something taught will be on the test should be rejected by any good teacher as being irrelevant – it reflects a classroom culture focused on testing rather than learning. Tests should grow from what is being taught, and what is taught should grow from who is being taught. If a test fits, then it might be useful; if not, then the tail is wagging the dog. Albert Einstein, writing about his own school experience, wrote:

---

[5] Steven Harrison, *The Happy Child, Changing The Heart of Education*, Boulder, CO: Sentient Publications, 2002. pp.16-17.

> ... one had to cram all this stuff into one's mind for the examinations, whether one liked it or not. This coercion had such a deterring effect that, after I had passed the final examination, I found the consideration of any scientific problems distasteful to me for an entire year.[6]

Most importantly, we need to question what relevance to the lives of children do the school's activities have? We too often forget that the real measurement of success in education is not what students can do and perform in school, but what they ultimately choose to do outside of school, what they take with them from the school.

When I was a principal I always wanted to consider what the student was experiencing in his or her life, and how was school either contributing to helping the student deal with life's challenges, or as I feared, how the school was serving to intensify life's challenges. Perhaps worst of all, was the student's experience in school mostly irrelevant to all of what was going on in his or her mind and heart? It was quite clear to me that if there was a disconnect, then no matter how well we were doing from the perspective of the regular standards, we were doing something wrong. I was very concerned about the disorder, the chaos, what my wife Chana always calls the *Tohu Vavohu* that confronted the student, what William James, in his famous phrase characterizing life, called a "buzzing, blooming confusion." What challenged me always was, how can we provide the tools, the wherewithal to students to deal with that?

Educating toward a changing world

Today's world is a radically different place than it was just thirty years ago. I am not talking about computers and the new math and a myriad of scientific data that we did not have then, but about the ways in which society is different. Are our schools radically different than they were thirty years ago? I sometimes suspect that we are going backwards to fill a nostalgic need to recreate a world gone by, one which may never have really existed except in our revisionist and ro-

---

[6] "Autobiographical Notes," in *Albert Einstein: Philosopher-Scientist,* Paul Schilpp, ed. (1951), pp. 17-19 © 1951 by the Library of Living Philosophers, Inc.

manticized conceptions of it. In this incredibly sophisticated and confusing world, it becomes increasingly important to reflect on whether we are providing the kind of education that will prepare young people to deal with all of this very sophisticated confusion.

Important questions that school leaders must ask themselves, despite the fact that they may be somewhat broad and nebulous, include: What is the nature of the school community that I want to develop and maintain? What are students that study at this school experiencing? How am I preparing my students for their futures?

Permit me to share with you some of the issues that energized me in creating a vision and program for the school that I was responsible for, what I viewed as the overpowering responsibility for the growth and social, emotional, spiritual and intellectual development of the hundreds of students who entered the doors of the school. I was first and foremost always troubled, perhaps haunted is a more appropriate word, by two fears:

A. Somehow I was wasting everyone's time and that I had not thought out clearly enough what we should be doing in this grand experiment called a Jewish high school. Not that we were not considered an excellent school by the regular, objective standards – in fact, by those standards we were doing very well, and I knew that if it were not the case, then we would have been out of business. But I always wondered that there must be better, perhaps much better ways, to do it.

B. That the school community did not genuinely and deeply care or relate to the issues that moved me, that energized me or that I thought should be energizing them.

Regarding the first, the opening line of *Kodachrome,* a Simon and Garfunkel song, echoed constantly in my head (and please forgive the language): "When I think back on all the crap I've learned in high school/ It's a wonder I can think at all." I wanted to make sure, in my extreme naiveté, in whichever way I could, that the students who studied in my school would not think like the first line in that song. Perhaps it was arrogant to believe that it was achievable, but I could not bear the thought that we may be wasting our students' precious time. Remember the commercial for the United Negro College Fund,

"A mind is a terrible thing to waste." The only difference is that the commercial was talking about kids who did not go to school.

To keep myself in line, I had tucked away in my drawer, one of the opening paragraphs from *A Catcher in the Rye.* Speaking through Holden Caulfield, at the very beginning of the book J.D. Salinger writes:

> Where I want to start telling is the day I left Pencey Prep. Pencey Prep is this school that's in Agerstown Pennsylvania. You probably heard of it. You've probably seen the ads anyway. They advertise in about a thousand magazines, always showing some hot-shot guy on a horse jumping over a fence. Like as if all you ever did at Pencey was play polo all the time. I never even once saw a horse anywhere near the place. And underneath the guy on the horse's picture, it always says: "Since 1888 we have been molding boys into splendid, clear-thinking young men." Strictly for the birds. They don't do any more molding at Pencey than they do at any other school. And I didn't know anybody there that was splendid and clear thinking and all. Maybe two guys. And they probably came to Pencey that way.

I always wondered whether the students who did well in our school, did well because of us or despite us. I believe that schools need to be a bit more careful when they promote themselves based on the outstanding academic performance of their academically outstanding students.

But mostly I was also driven by the second fear, about the expectations, concerns and values of the students, the parents, the school community. Did parents really care at all about the issues that I thought about constantly, the kinds of things that I wanted to energize the dynamic and the climate at the school? They certainly cared very much about the overall development of their children but there always seemed to be so much more focus on the more external measurements – grades, SAT scores, performance in drama or debate or basketball, acceptance to an Ivy League university, or the ability to deliver a *devar Torah* at the Shabbat table – as if the programmed performance of that child in front of family and guests was some kind of important measurement of something. And while these are all important, they were certainly not the issues that energized me to want to be in education. And if these were the concerns of the parents, how different were the values of their children? Of course, there are profound distinctions between children and their parents, but they are so often reflections of one another.

Toward a better Jewish education

In Jewish tradition, learning is indeed a means but it is also an end unto itself; the value of the intellectual experience is the experience itself. The study of Torah, writes Abraham Joshua Heschel, is the process of being involved in dialogue with God. Learning is not only preparation for life, but it is life – in many senses, the supreme experience of living; the climax of existence.

In a well-known homiletic passage (Tractate Niddah 30b), Rabbi Simlai explained that an embryo is taught all the Torah from beginning to end, but as soon as it sees light, an angel approaches, slaps it on the mouth and causes it to forget all the Torah completely. Rav Soloveitchik, in a lecture at the University of Pennsylvania, examined this passage:

> There is an obvious question: If the angel makes the baby forget everything he taught it, why did he bother to teach the embryo at all? Rabbi Simlai wanted to tell us that when a Jew studies Torah he is confronted with something which is not foreign and extraneous, but rather intimate and already familiar, because he has already studied it. And that knowledge is part of him. He studies, in effect, his own stuff. Learning then is the recollection of something familiar. The Jew studying Torah is like the amnesia victim who tries to reconstruct from fragments the beautiful world he once experienced. In other words, by learn-

> ing Torah, man returns to his own self; man finds himself.[7]

Do our day schools come close to conveying a relationship with learning that reflects the Rav's description? Is such a goal somehow built in to the actual school program?

I have just described some of the issues in education in general, and the place of learning in Jewish tradition. Shouldn't the most prominent among goals of day schools be to nurture enthusiasm for study, for nurturing a learning framework that works to encourage connection to the material and creates personal meaning? What would an educational program designed to recognize enthusiasm for study and commitment to learning, even without concomitant achievement, look like? What sort of assessments and evaluations could we create that would set the standards for and reward asking good questions even more than repeating cookie-cutter answers?

These questions become more compelling when applied to Jewish schools, for indeed if one of the goals of a Jewish day school is to nurture the commitment and enthusiasm of the most committed students to Judaism – to Jewish life, to the Jewish community – are they approaching it the right way? And if it is not happening for the committed day school community, how can we even dream about reaching the uncommitted?

Learning for, and within, Jewish life

Judaism is a living tradition and is dynamic as a result of its oral traditions, but the foundation, the direction and prescription, the framework for this living tradition is found in texts. And that is why we study them. The Biblical and Rabbinic literature lay the foundation for the entire experience of Judaism. They are the basis and source of the Hebrew language, of literature, Jewish ethics, Jewish wisdom, Jewish prayer, the Jewish legal system, the Jewish religion, ritual, Jewish history, and all of Jewish culture.

But learning must be rooted in life. In order to flourish, to borrow from David Hartman, learning requires living situations and living contexts out of which the text can speak. (The same is, of course, true

---

7 Rabbi Joseph B. Soloveitchik, "Redemption, Prayer and Talmud Torah," in *Tradition* 17:2 (Spring 1978), p. 69.

for general studies.) It seems that the best, or perhaps the only, way to create a living situation in school is for it to relate to the living situation outside of school. We need to build our program around what is going in the student's mind and heart, what moves him. Here are some of the specific issues that I believe educators need to consider (some of the following questions are based on some writings of Michael Rosenak):

- Can we, in Jewish schools, live with the notion that good questions almost never have as good an answer?
- Are we aware of the stages of religious development in children?
- Are we sensitive to theories of psychological and moral development and their applicability to Jewish issues?
- Are children naturally spiritual or must they be socialized into religious culture? Are we nurturing something that is inherent or does educating for spirituality demand that we ask of students to reach outside of themselves?
- Is our aim in Jewish studies/religious education to familiarize our students with obligation, to encourage commitment, to bestow meaning? How do we accomplish this via texts and experiences?
- How do we balance the competing needs of Jewish literacy and meaning? How can we infuse that literacy with meaning?
- What weight does the fundamental need for literacy and substance in content have vis-à-vis other values and goals in the school?
- By which criteria do we choose topics and texts for study?
- If the goals of Jewish studies differ from those of general studies, do we have adequate methods of measuring success in Jewish studies? How will those differences be understood, in terms of valuing that learning, by students and their parents?
- Should the Jewish agenda of the school limit content that is studied in general studies classes?
- What will be the relationship between Jewish and general studies? Will they be two ships passing in the night, two competing world views, or tightly integrated?
- How do we bridge the gaps between students and their teachers, who often inhabit a very different world?

- What are our criteria for choosing Jewish studies faculty? Do we prefer academic expertise, pedagogical excellence, outstanding modeling, or some other criteria?
- Is doctrinal conformity amongst the faculty required, or desired? Does that factor weigh more heavily than other criteria?
- What kinds of policies need to be in place regarding people and institutions of different religious conviction, in Judaism and outside of Judaism? How does a school arrive at a modicum of reason and policy that communicates tolerance and at the same time promotes particularism?
- How do we determine the balance between encouraging free thinking in the school and fostering commitment to Jewish tradition? How should the inherent tension between authority and autonomy be dealt with?
- What is needed in terms of teacher training, professional development and curriculum construction to even make better teachers succeed?

The Jewish school meets the outside world

Would we answer these questions differently in the post-modern world, dominated by hedonistic individualism on one side and authoritarian spiritualism on the other, than we would in a society motivated by scientific rationalism? Accommodating a world which places extreme emphasis on achievement, wealth and prestige, do we run the risk of assuring ourselves a materially comfortable but spiritually sterile future? When considering what is happening in the broader lives of our students and the surrounding culture, we face the additional challenge of whether to work within that culture or to present a counter-culture, at it were, to the prevailing values. Is it part of the school's mandate to educate the community – effectively creating a sub-community within the broader one? Robert Frost's counsel, in the poem, Mending Wall, comes to mind: "before I built a wall I'd ask to know what I was walling in or walling out."

There are topics and approaches to issues that many would consider out-of-bounds in Jewish schools. Consider evolution in one school, sexual counseling in another, Biblical criticism in a third, comparative religion in yet one more. Are there subjects that should not be broached, perspectives that should not be taught? Should students be exposed to the broadest array of challenges they will face, and learn to deal with those within whatever ideological framework the school establishes? Is that too risky a proposition?

Does knowledge of general culture enhance our students' ability to understand and appreciate Jewish texts and vice versa? Rabbi Aharon Lichtenstein, the *Rosh Ha-Yeshiva* of Yeshivat Har Etzion, claims that general culture can take you places that Jewish sources may not be able to. Culture, according to Rav Lichtenstein, provides or enriches our ability to understand, appreciate, and deal with our personal, communal issues, sensitivity to the human condition and some assistance in coping with it. Culture instills in us a sense of the moral, psychological and metaphysical complexity of life. He argues that one can have a much more refined understanding of Midrash or *Tanakh* if one has an eye for literature.

For example, Elisha, seeking prophetic inspiration, requests that he be brought a minstrel; and when the minstrel played, the hand of the Lord came upon him. Maimonides comments that the spirit of prophecy does not descend upon one who is melancholy but comes as a result of joyousness. Asks Rav Lichtenstein, if inspiration can be drawn from pipes and harps can it not be drawn from poetry as well? The fusion of knowledge and power, insight and inspiration provided by great literature enables us to enrich our spiritual lives. Study of general culture, he claims, can become a vehicle for enhancing our Torah existence.[8]

Closing reflection

So much of what we do is the product of inertia, it's the way we've always done it or the way it has always been done. Even worse is when those unquestioned practices become dogma – we *must* do it this way because that's the way it has always been done. That dogma stifles and inhibits any possibility for change and growth, and we are left with practices whose rationale has long been forgotten. Remember Rav Ḥanokh of Alexander's comment that the real slavery of Israel in Egypt was that they learned to endure it.

---

8 "Torah and General Culture: Confluence and Conflict", in *Judaism's Encounter with Other Cultures, Rejecton or Integration*?, ed. Jacob J. Schacter (Northvale NJ, 1997) p. 252

I close as I opened, with two anecdotes. These are both from former students, both of whom came to a Jewish high school in the 11th grade and accomplished in two years what we would hope all our students could have achieved in twelve years. Both are students who came from the world of general culture and a general school background and advanced extraordinarily in their Jewish learning and identity. And for both, their Jewish school experience had a profound impact on them. Interestingly, their most effective mode of expression was through the medium of general culture.

The first story one is about a young man who, on the last day of school in the 11th grade, walked into my office and very discreetly handed me a tape saying, "here, this is for you." After which he turned and left the room. It piqued my curiosity, so I played the tape right away. It contained one song sung by the popular group, Crosby, Stills and Nash. The lyrics which caught my attention are:

> Look around me, I can see my life before me,
> Running rings around the way it used to be.
> I am older now, I have more than what I wanted
> But I wish that I had started long before I did.
> And there's so much time to make up
> Everywhere you turn,
> Time we have wasted on the way.

I was moved. I had never heard the song before.

The second story is about a young woman who also joined us in the eleventh grade for very unusual reasons. She also came into my office on the last day of class and handed me a note, and it read like this:

> I'm just writing to thank you for the opportunity you gave me to learn Torah and be in an atmosphere of warmth and learning. I've learned a lot about Torah, friendship, and communal responsibility, and I've got to credit it to the school and its administration. Many of the values and priorities I have now were at one time non-existent. The school has really molded my lifestyle, and I say that exclusive of NCSY. Although NCSY has been the single most important religious

> catalyst and atmosphere I've had the honor of belonging to, I learned from many years of *kumsitzes* and *zemirot* that behind all of the fire and emotion must lie a strong, solid foundation of knowledge. That can only be achieved through *Talmud Torah*, and religion can only perpetuate with this as its basis. The school gave me the desire for this knowledge and helped me gain part of it – I've still got a long way to go.
>
> Khalil Gibran said it best:
>
> "The teacher who walks in the shadow of the temple, among his followers, gives not of his wisdom but rather of his faith and his loving kindness. If he is indeed wise he does not bid you enter the house of his wisdom, but rather leads you to the threshold of your own mind."
>
> Thank you once again. I hope one day I will be able to repay you.

These two stories gave me a much different, but more intelligible and more concrete understanding of the homiletic statement of Rabba bar Rav Huna (Tractate Shabbat 31a). There are inner doors and outer doors to the treasure of wisdom. If we want our students to reach the treasure, we must be careful to give them the keys to the outer door as well as the inner one, lest we deny them access to that treasure.

Universalism, Particularism and "The Dignity of Difference:" Pedagogical and curricular implications

Moshe Sokolow

Prologue: Philosophy and Pedagogy

To live as a Jew in general, and as an Orthodox Jew in particular, is often to be caught between contradictory or competing principles. We believe, for instance, that God created Adam in a *tzelem Elohim* and that implies a measure of equality to all human beings. On the other hand, we consider ourselves a "singular people," (*am segulah*) implying a difference between Jews and non-Jews. We also affirm the principle of whereby obedience to the word of God, manifested in the Torah and its *halakhic* interpretation, can transform the ordinary and mundane into the holy and sublime. This, in turn, implies that Jews who abide by *halakhah* stand apart from non-observant Jews.

What should be the attitude of Jews to non-Jews who share with them their essential "divine image" but lack the singularity of election? What should be the attitude of *halakhically* observant Jews towards non-observant Jews who possess the ingredient of election but fail to exercise their option for enhanced sanctification? Are these differences qualitative or quantitative? Should they be regarded as indications of distinctiveness or of superiority?

The philosophical substratum of this presentation is informed by the several principles alluded to above.

First, is the fundamental belief that every human being possesses a *tzelem Elohim*. We share with all mankind our origin as a species and every human being is entitled, as such, to some elemental consideration.

We take our cue in this regard from the Mishnah in Avot (3:14):

> He [R. Akiva] was accustomed to saying: Man is beloved [of God] because he was created in a form. Greater love was [evinced] by informing him of his

> creation in a form, to wit: "In a divine/majestic image did He create man" (Gen. 9:6).[1]

Second, is the belief that the difference between Jews and non-Jews is not an essential one. We became an *am segulah* by virtue of our greater service of God, not on account of any fundamental, qualitative distinction.

Third, it is the ingredient of *kedushah*, sanctity, that distinguishes observant from non-observant Jews, and that the characteristic property of *kedushah* is separation. *Ḥazal* noted that *Kedoshim tihyu* means be separate; they did not say "be isolated".

In pedagogical terms, we take our cue from two recent monographs on the subject of our relationship to the "other." The first is an essay entitled: "Judaism and Other Religions; an Orthodox Perspective," by Yeshiva University Professor Alan Brill[2] and the second is *The Dignity of Difference* by Chief Rabbi Jonathan Sacks.[3] From these two erudite and forthright scholars, we shall adopt the particular stance that they

---

1 Our translation of "divine/majestic image" (taking the Hebrew words *tzelem Elohim* as a noun and adjective, rather than a construct of two nouns) is justified by comparison with the Arabic translation of Saadiah Gaon and the commentary of R. David Kimḥi. Saadiah (882-942) explains in his commentary that "[God] made man in His form in respect of sovereignty and dominion, not in respect of physiognomy or appearance" (Moses Zucker: Perushei Rav Saadiah Gaon le-Bereishit (New York, 1984), Hebrew p. 257, Arabic p. 53).

R. David Kimḥi (1160-1235) treats the word Elohim in Ezekiel 1:1 as an adjective, commenting:

> This means great and spectacular visions, since the custom of Scripture, when it wishes to make something grand, is to liken it to the divine. Such as: "an enormously large city" (Jonah 3:3), "majestic mountains" (Ps. 36:7), "lofty cedars" (Ps. 80:11), "deep gloom" (Jer. 2:31), or "a blazing flame" (Song 8:6).

Webster, too, defines "divine" (adj.) as "supremely good, superb."

This rendition has the added advantage of obviating the need to "apologize" for the conventional "image of God" with its concomitant philosophical and theological complexities.

2 http://www.bc.edu/research/cjl/meta-elements/texts/cjrelations/resources/articles/Brill.htm [reconfirmed 12/01/05]

3 Subtitled: How to avoid the clash of civilizations (London, New York: Continuum, 2002).

advocate towards other religions, which we shall endeavor to translate into curricular and instructional priorities for modern Orthodox day schools.[4]

The objective of this paper is to offer a sampling of pertinent sources that bear upon this dilemma and propose methodological and curricular guidelines for their contemplation and implementation. In the final analysis, the students will render their own judgments. No matter how well (or loudly) we teach (or preach), we are but one of many separate and often dissonant influences on the development and maturation of a religious personality. Parents are such an influence, peers are another and the culture, with its pervasive and often pernicious media, is a third.[5]

It is our responsibility to provide our students with authentic and credible alternatives from which to fashion their individual attitudes and dispositions.[6]

Caveat: Precedent and Prospect

It is *not* the objective of this presentation to make a convincing argument for having Orthodox day schools educate towards a universal-

4 Non-observant Jews are unaffected by part of the dilemma because they generally do not acknowledge the compulsory nature of *halakhah*, while the so-called "ultra" Orthodox limit their contacts with either non-Jews or non-Orthodox Jews. We assume that modern Orthodox students, as a consequence of their modernity, have, and will both increase and intensify, contact with non-Jews and non-Orthodox Jews. In certain respects, then, this didactic dilemma is quintessentially modern Orthodox.

5 The tone of debate in the Orthodox community, of late, is particularly shrill when the subject is Israeli politics. Right and left, right and wrong, pillory one another relentlessly, and the implementation of the disengagement in Gaza brought us dangerously close to the renewal of internecine hostilities that have been latent since the handshake in the Rose garden in September of 1993. While Israel concerns itself with the preservation of order in military ranks due to partisan rabbinical pronouncements on defying orders, we in the US need to be concerned about an outbreak of the same kind of public demagoguery that poisoned the air around the time of the assassination of Yitzhak Rabin, z"l.

6 See Yisrael Rich's "Assessing Emerging Identity among Religious High School Students: Reflections on the Israeli Experience " in this volume for a further exploration of identity development in adolescents.

istic approach to the relationship between Judaism and other religions. Such arguments (like those of Brill and Sacks, cited above) exist and do not require my approbation. The objective of this presentation is to provide schools that are already persuaded by these arguments with advice on how to best integrate such an education into their curricula and instructional practices. Such Biblical, Talmudic-Midrashic, Medieval and Modern sources as we may cite in the course of this paper should be regarded as proof texts for the *inception* of the proposed study rather than for its *conception*.

Preliminary Curricular Guidelines

A. Defining Curriculum

Our preferred definition of curriculum is:

> All the *learning* which is *planned and guided* by the school, whether it is carried on in groups or individually, inside or outside the school.[7]

From this definition, operative pedagogical and didactic consequences ensue.

(1) The emphasis on "learning" (as opposed to the more traditional [Tylerian] formula of "instruction") testifies to the replacement of the "transmission of knowledge" model with something more akin to the "experiential" model.[8]

(2) The qualification "planned and guided" indicates that we have to specify in advance what we are seeking to achieve, how we are to go about its achievement, and how we will determine how much of it has been achieved and how well.

(3) The propinquity of curriculum to "school" is a constant reminder that we are obliged to operate within the real confines of a school, both spatial and temporal. The "school year," "school day," and

7 John Kerr quoted in Kelly, A. V.: *The Curriculum. Theory and Practice* (4e, London: Paul Chapman, 1983; 1999).

8 See Roland Barth: *Learning by Heart* (San Francisco, 2001), 32 ff., 48 ff.

"school building" are no less defining and delineating than subject matter, instructional material, and tools of assessment.

This definition of curriculum is accompanied by a preferred definition of schoolwork:

> In sum, the business of schools is to produce work that engages students, that is so compelling that students persist when they experience difficulties, and that is so challenging that students have a sense of accomplishment, of satisfaction – indeed, of delight – when they successfully accomplish the tasks assigned.[9]

B. Choosing a theory of curriculum development

(1) Structure

I have elected to use the "Paideia" structure, which is intrinsically more compatible with traditional day-school curricular practices. According to the Paideia model, one stipulates:

- the "organized knowledge" to be acquired,
- the "intellectual skills" of acquisition and analysis, and
- the "enlarged understanding of ideas and values" to be derived from the application of those skills to that body of knowledge.[10]

(2) Content

The specific application of curriculum that we have chosen is entitled "Understanding by Design," which features a tripartite process of development called "backward design":

- Identify desired results – consisting of enduring understandings, essential questions, knowledge and basic skills;
- Determine acceptable evidence – via informal checks, observation and dialogue, quizzes and tests, academic prompts, performance tasks and projects;

---

[9] Phillip Schlechty: *Inventing Better Schools* (San Francisco: Jossey-Bass, 2001), 58.

[10] Mortimer Adler: *The Paideia Proposal: An Educational Manifesto* (Macmillan, 1982).

- Plan learning experiences and instruction.[11]

C. Implementation: Selecting the Proof Texts

Textually, we begin at three junctures that intersect with the three philosophical principles outlined above:

1. The principle of the essential equality of all mankind intersects with the study of Sefer Bereishit, and with selected *mizmorim* of Tehillim;
2. The principle of quantitative election intersects with the study of Sefer Shemot, Megillat Ruth, and with selections from *Nevi-im Aḥaronim*;
3. The principle of elevated *kedushah* through the observance of *mitzvot* intersects with the study of the *sidrah* of Kedoshim and with portions of Sefer Devarim.

Bereishit

1. Creation

A reading of the story of creation based on *peshat* yields a universalistic message. Life does not begin with Avraham, the first Jew, but with Adam, the first human. It does not begin in the Land of Israel, but in the extraterritorial terrain called Eden. Adam and Eve are not *any* two people; they are the progenitors of the entire human race. Their sin of disobedience and expulsion from the Garden, as well as Cain's commission of fratricide, constitute deeds of universal proportions and universal consequences.

This point can be reinforced in the classroom by studying the Mishnah in Sanhedrin (4:5), which refers to the these stories while

11 Grant Wiggins, Jay McTighe: *Understanding by Design* (Alexandria Va., 1998). Cf. http://www.ascd.org/ASCD/pdf/books/mctighe2004_intro.pdf [reconfirmed 12/01/05].

"Enduring understandings" go beyond discrete facts or skills to focus on larger concepts, principles, or processes, while "essential questions" go to the heart of a discipline, recur naturally throughout one's learning and in the history of a field, and raise other important questions. The success of a curriculum is proportional to the degree to which the "essential" questions it raises find their answers in those particular understandings that meet the definition of "enduring."

prescribing the manner in which court officials are required to admonish witnesses in trials for capital crimes. In order to ensure that the witnesses consider the enormous consequences of their testimony, they are told:

> Therefore was solitary man created, to inform us that whoever destroys but one life[12] it is as though he destroyed an entire world; and whoever sustains but one life, it is as though he sustained an entire world. And in order to maintain peaceful relations among human beings, lest one say to another, "My father is greater than your father," and to preempt the argument of the heretics that there are multiple authorities in heaven. And to relate the greatness of the King of kings of kings, the Holy One, blessed be He: A man may cast one hundred coins in the same mold and they will all resemble one another, while the King of kings of kings, the Holy One, blessed be He, casts every human being in the [single] image of Adam and no two are identical. It is therefore incumbent on each and every person to say, "The world was created for me!"

2. The Flood

The story of the flood, too, is clearly universal in scope and consequence. In this context, I would suggest that the teacher lead the students through the narrative highlighting the way in which the destruction caused by the flood reverses the sequence in which the world was created and that the restoration of life on earth after the flood replicates the sequence of the original creation[13], thereby lending additional emphasis to its universal proportions. The moral of the story,

---

[12] The addition, here, of the adjective "Israelite" is contraindicated by the context and unattested to in reliable manuscripts, including the text of this Mishnah that accompanies Maimonides' holographic commentary on it. There are, however, alternate Midrashic sources in which the word appears to be authentic. Cf. E.E. Urbach, Tarbiz 40 (1971), 268-284.

[13] E.g., after the flood, like in the "beginning," a dry earth emerges from within a watery abyss, followed by the reappearance of vegetation, the luminaries, animal life and, finally, man.

I believe, is captured in the title of the well-known song: "It's a small world after all." The fate we share as inhabitants of the same planet is a consequence of our common mortality; any injury done to any limb or organ of the "majestic image" will necessarily harm the entire body.

From this universal perspective, it is easier to understand why the key creation idiom, *tzelem Elohim*, reappears after the flood in the specific context of the laws of homicide (Genesis 9:6):

> Whoever sheds human blood shall [forfeit] his own blood to be shed by humans, for [God] created humankind in a divine/majestic image.[14]

God's sanction against homicide is universal precisely because human life has no "particular" value.[15] As the Mishnah (above) stipulates: "Whoever destroys but one life, it is as though he destroyed an entire world."

3. The Tower of "Babel"

The interpretation of this narrative offers a distinct exegetical challenge. It is situated between the universal narratives of creation and the flood, and the particular narratives of the patriarchs. To which genre does it belong?

Without delving excessively into the text,[16] we would note, again, the advantage of viewing this narrative as universal (cf. Rashi), rather than particular (Ramban). Specifically, we would recommend balancing their Aggadic interpretation (i.e., an attempt on the part of mankind to displace God) with a more *peshat* oriented approach (cf. Ibn Ezra and Rashbam), which sees the crime in their failure to abide by God's post-diluvian imperative to "be fruitful, multiply and replenish

---

14 While earlier (2:7), the Torah plays on the assonance of Adam and *adamah*, here it plays on its assonance with *dam*. A combination of the two yields the midrashic notion that Adam was formed of reddish clay.

15 See M. Sokolow: "Discovering the Biblical Value of Human Life," Ten Da`at X (1997), 41 ff.

16 See M. Sokolow: "The Bible and Religious Education," Studies in Jewish Education 4 (1989), 42 ff., particularly 54-62: "The Tower of Babel, A Model for Coordinated Inquiry."

the world" (Genesis 9:1), emphasizing the original occurrence of this instruction to Adam and Eve (1:28).

As noted above (2), the flood narrative deliberately incorporates themes and terms that originate in the narrative of creation, adding to our impression that the tower narrative, too, is part and parcel of the universal story of all mankind and not, yet, the particular story of just one nation, tribe or family.

Tehillim

The majesty of humanity that is inherent in creation is featured in Psalm 8:

> When I see Your heavens, fashioned by Your fingers – the moon and stars that You fixed in place; What is mortal man that You are mindful of him, humankind that You take note of him? You have made him slightly less than divine, and crowned him with honor and glory. You have given him dominion over Your handiwork, laying the world at his feet.

The impressive and unforgettable lyrical nature of Psalms provides a valuable contrast with often dry, monotonous prose. Where the Torah merely speaks, however eloquently, Tehillim rhapsodizes. Since we aspire to influence our students' affect along with their cognition, we should utilize Biblical poetry as a counterpoint to its prose, just as its own authors and editors sought to forestall the boredom of their readers through the judicious alternation of literary styles and genres.[17]

I would make the following methodological, didactic recommendation. Arrange the verses in Tehillim in one column, phrase by phrase (according to the system of "didactic transcription"), and challenge the students to match each poetic Psalm phrase with a corresponding prose passage from the Torah. Have them consider whether the

---

17 See M. Sokolow: "Sa`adiah Gaon's Prolegomenon to the Book of Psalms," PAAJR vol. LI (1984), 146.

correspondences are exact, where they differ, and whether there is a significant alteration or addition to the Torah narrative in Tehillim.[18]

Shemot

The principle of election, as we have noted above, derives from the revelation at Sinai. Immediately prior to the revelation itself, God declares His purpose (Exodus 19:5-6):

> Now, if you will obey me and keep my covenant and be my treasure among the peoples – for the entire earth is mine. [You shall then be unto me a kingdom of priests and a special nation…]

In this regard, we take our cue from R. Ovadiah Seforno (Italy; 1475-1550), who comments:

> Although the entire human race is more valuable to me than any of the lower order creatures – because man alone is the intended [i.e., central] one, as the rabbis said: "Man is beloved because he was created in a form" – in any event, you will be my most select of them all… and the distinction between you is quantitative; for the entire land is indeed mine, and the righteous among the nations of the world are undoubtedly dear to me as well.

Seforno's point – stimulated, no doubt, by the ethos of the Italian Renaissance in which he lived – is supported by a well-known Aggadic passage in the Talmud (Avodah Zarah 2b):

---

18 The result should look like this:

Bereishit	**Tehillim**
"… and rule the fish of the sea, the birds of the sky …" (Gen. 1:28)	"You have made him master over Your handiwork …" (Ps. 8:7)

> The [nations of the world] said before God: Lord of the universe, did you offer [the Torah] to us and did we reject it? How could they so argue? Does it not state: "The Lord came from Sinai and shone forth from Seir," and, "God came from the Yemen [i.e., South];" what did He seek in Seir and in Paran? R. Yohanan said: This teaches us that God proffered [the Torah] to every nation and culture and no one accepted it, until He arrived at Israel who accepted it.

This Aggadah implies that the Torah could have been revealed to any national or ethnic group; no particular, qualitative prerequisite was set for it.[19] Its acceptance by the Jewish people provides us with a special, treasured relationship with God, but not one that could not be enjoyed by any human being who was willing to accept its yoke. Indeed, the entire concept of conversion rests on the *a priori* assumption that all human beings are essentially eligible to receive the Torah.

Megillat Ruth

There is no need to belabor the relevance of the story of Ruth to the essential eligibility of all people to accept the Torah. I would, nevertheless, like to offer an observation that frequently goes overlooked.

Towards the close of the first chapter, Naomi implores her daughters-in-law to leave her and to return to their homes and families. Orpah relents and returns. When Ruth refuses to abandon Naomi and "cleaves to her" (Ruth 1:14), Naomi utilizes Orpah as an object lesson, saying: "See, your sister-in-law is returning… why don't you follow her?" (1:15). The ellipsis is telling; the full text reads: "See, your sister-in-law is returning *to her people and to her gods*, why don't you follow her?" In other words, Naomi has no problem with Orpah returning to a life of idol worship and neither does the text denounce or chastise her for offering that choice.

The point overlooked is that, from Naomi's perspective, it is not Orpah alone who would have been better off returning to Moab; it is Ruth, too. Indeed, this verse highlights the fact that on the eve of her

[19] While the nations declined to receive the Torah, *Ḥazal* still teach us that the Torah was "given in seventy languages" (Shabbat 88b), not in Hebrew alone.

conversion to Judaism, Ruth was regarded by Naomi as an idolatress, yet this did not militate against her; she still became the ancestress of the Messiah.

> [The angels said to Lot:] "Arise and take your two daughters who are found." R. Toviah bar Yitzḥak said: This refers to two "finds," Ruth the Moabitess and Naamah the Amonitess. R. Yitzḥak said: "I have found my servant, David" (Ps. 89:21); where did I find him? In Sedom![20]

The Aggadah capitalizes on Ruth's Moabite ancestry to make a point about not denigrating gentiles – even coarse idolaters – because one can never know who might descend from them. Viewed symbolically, the Aggadah is asserting that the ultimate redemption of the Jewish people would not have been possible without the active participation of non-Jews. King David was descended from Ruth, who was herself descended from one of the daughters of Lot who, to recall, bore a child to her father after their evacuation from Sedom. Even incest does not disqualify gentiles from playing a positive role in the unfurling of God's universal plan.[21]

Nevi-im Aḥaronim

Prophetic eschatology also attests to the universality of Judaism. We remarked earlier (cf. Shemot) on the essential eligibility of all mankind to receive the Torah and that *Tanakh* is not critical of idola-

---

[20] Variations on this theme are found in the Talmud, as well: cf. Baba Bata 91b.

[21] The Midrash records a similar theme apropos of Yehudah's "affair" with Tamar:

> The tribes were busy with the sale of Yoseph, Yoseph was busy with his sackcloth and fasting, Reuven was busy with his sackcloth and fasting, Yaakov was busy with his sackcloth and fasting, Yehudah was busy taking a wife, and The Holy One Blessed be He was busy creating the light of the Messiah. (Bereishit Rabbah 25)

This theme may also be behind the declaration (Yoma 22b):

> No one can be appointed to oversee communal affairs unless a box of reptiles is suspended behind him. In the case that he grows arrogant he will be told: Look behind you!

ters for idolatry, *per se* (cf. Ruth). To these points we now add the observation that in the eschatological visions of the prophets for the "end of days," mankind will yet have the opportunity it once declined (and even disdained) to realize the truth of Torah and embrace it. [22]

- Yeshayah 2:2 (=Mikha 2:1)
  And many peoples shall go and say: 'Come ye, and let us go up to the mountain of the Lord, to the house of the God of Jacob; and He will teach us of His ways, and we will walk in His paths'...

- Yeshayah 56:6-7
  Also the aliens, that join themselves to the Lord, to minister unto Him, and to love the name of the Lord, to be His servants... Even them will I bring to My holy mountain, and make them joyful in My house of prayer...

- Zephaniah 3:9
  For then will I turn to the peoples a pure language that they may all call upon the name of the Lord, to serve Him with one consent.

Kedoshim

The *locus classicus* of *kedushah* is Vayikra 19:2, "Speak to the Israelites and tell them be *kedoshim*, for I, your God, am *kadosh*," and the operative definition of *kedushah* is provided by Rashi, "separate yourselves

---

[22] Cf. Devarim 4:19:

> Lest you raise your eyes heavenward and you see the sun, moon and starts, all the heavenly hosts, and stray and bow to them, which A-donai your God has assigned for all the nations under the heavens.

On the phrase "which the Lord, your God, has assigned to all the nations," Rashi first suggests that [He assigned them] as luminaries, but adds, alternatively, as deities. While Rashi adds that God permitted them to worship celestial bodies as an excuse to punish them, Rashbam, offering the same pair of interpretations, explains the sanction of such worship on the grounds of His indifference towards them.

Also cf. Mikha 4:5: "For all the nations will each go with the name of their god..." While Rashi, again, interprets it as a pretext for their destruction, Radak comments that they are not eternally incorrigible.

from lewdness and from [all manner of] transgression." The proof text cited earlier for the principle of quantitative election (Shemot 19: 5-6), however, can serve for the principle of elevated *kedushah* through the observance of *mitzvot*, as well: "You shall then be unto Me a kingdom of priests and a special nation..."

Rather than focus on personal sanctity, I should like to draw our attention to other forms of sanctity – sanctity of time and sanctity of place.

Let us first point out that both Shabbat and the *Moadim* come with two equal sets of prescriptive detail: national and universal. Each version of the Decalogue provides a different reason for observing Shabbat: the particular one, to commemorate the exodus from Egypt, and a universal one, to recall creation. Each of the three pilgrimage festivals similarly has a particular reason – the exodus, the journey through the wilderness and the revelation of the law – as well as one marking the cycle of agriculture, universal to all peoples in the region.

Even when it comes to the matter of marking the New Year, our tradition records two opinions regarding the precise timing of creation: Nisan and Tishrei. Remarkably, while it allocates the former to the national purpose of assigning years to the reign of a Jewish king, it is the latter, the universal New Year, that we observe as Rosh ha-Shanah.

With respect to the sanctity of place, R. Moshe Avigdor Amiel has written:

> The aim of our nationalism is internationalism. Nationalism is the means, but internationalism is the goal. Nationalism requires a homeland and a racial uniqueness; but we lack these elements. You see, our history did not begin in a homeland; on the contrary, it began with the command "Go out of your country and your birthplace." Long after Avraham obeyed the command and settled in Eretz Yisrael, when he was an old man, our first Patriarch bade his chief servant, Eliezer, to go "to my country and birthplace," meaning to Ur Kasdim in Mesopotamia. There was his homeland; his (and our) Promised Land, where he lived, was elsewhere. Nor are we a special race,

> members of a particular (superior) group or society; we are only descendants of an individual designated in Scripture as "one:" "Look unto Avraham your father and Sarah who bore you for I called him 'one'" (Yeshayah 51:2).[23]

Instructional Postscript – Methodological Implications

Universalism does not manifest itself only in the choice and sequence of Biblical, Talmudic and Rabbinic subject matter; it carries serious implications for the instructional methodologies we utilize, as well. Whereas a particularistic approach, for example, would limit discussion to Jewish sources and commentaries (even, perhaps, to Orthodox sources and commentaries), a universalistic approach would tolerate – if not actually embrace – non-Orthodox and even non-Jewish sources and commentaries, too, ranging from ancient Near Eastern literature and history to modern historical and archaeological studies, to literary criticism. As the modern Orthodox Bible scholar, Moshe David Cassuto, observed:

> The intention [of Tanakh] was to create a new culture, principally and fundamentally opposed to the culture [of the ancient Near East], while still drawing upon them and receiving sustenance from them in all aspects of material day to day life, as well as in regard to anything which did not contradict those fundamental principles.[24]

Here, too, we find that medieval authorities, in spite of their relatively limited resources, anticipated the moderns. Rambam asserted:

> The knowledge of those [pagan] attitudes and activities is a prime source for providing the rationale of *mitzvot*, for the basis of our entire Torah, and the

[23] Light for an Age of Confusion: Viewing the 20th Century according to the Torah (le-Nevukhei ha-Tekufah) vol. II (Jerusalem, 1996), 43.

[24] M. D. Cassuto: *Safrut Mikra-it ve-Safrut Cenaanit* (Jerusalem, 1975), 5.

> axis on which it rotates, is the elimination of those attitudes from our thoughts and of all traces [of those activities] from our reality.[25]

Moshe Ibn Ezra, author of a treatise on Hebrew poetics, wrote:

> In citing the Arabic Quran, I have paid no attention to the enmity adopted by certain opinions among the halakhists of our generation, because I have seen that the greatest halakhists and [Kalam] philosophers, including R. Saadiah Gaon and R. Hai Gaon, have relied upon it when seeking assistance in elucidating obscurities in prophetic literature. Likewise [they consulted] Christian commentaries, in spite of all their drawbacks.[26]

Rav Kook, in a distinctive, yet characteristic fashion, wrote:

> Is it not well know that among the ancients there were people who knew of God; prophets, spiritual giants, (including) Methushelaḥ, Ḥanokh, Shem, Ever, etc.?
>
> Is it conceivable that they had no influence on their contemporaries, despite being eclipsed by the activities of Eitan ha-Ezraḥi, i.e., Abraham?
>
> How could their influence have left no impression at all? Their works must have resembled those of the Torah![27]

---

[25] Guide for the Perplexed III:29.

[26] *Sefer ha-Iyyunim veha-Diyyunim* ed. Abraham S. Halkin (Jerusalem, 1975), 227. [The original Judeo-Arabic text is entitled: כתאב אלמחאצ'רה ואלמד'אכרה.] The opposition of (unnamed) Talmudists to the scientific study of Hebrew grammar and philology is attested to by Yonah Ibn Jannaḥ in his *Introduction to Sefer ha-Rikmah*) ed. Wilenski, p. 11).

[27] *Eider ha-Yakar* (Jerusalem, 1967), 52. Elsewhere, however, Rav Kook reveals a more polemical reason for this study:

The use of such sources for purposes of comparison and contrast is relevant to a proper contextual understanding of our own sources, and vital to the educational process by which we seek to insure that while our students participate in non-Jewish society and culture they are equipped with the ability to recognize and filter out those elements that are inimical to the Jewish faith.

R. Moshe Avigdor Amiel writes in a similar fashion:

> Historians and scholars have searched antiquity and found proof that many of the Torah's laws and statutes were known to other nations before the Torah was given to Israel. With this, however, there is no refutation of our faith; on the contrary, it strengthens our belief about "the souls that they [Avraham and Sarah] made in Ḥaran." Avraham was the pillar of benevolence and mercy, which form the essence of Judaism and the root of its contribution to the world. Noaḥ was also commanded to abide by laws and set up courts of justice; thus his contemporaries knew of the principle of justice even if they chose to ignore it.[28]

> It is necessary to study all the wisdoms in the world, all ways of life, all different cultures, along with the ethical systems and religions of all nations and languages, so that, with greatness of soul, one will know how to purify them all. [*Arpelei Tohar*, 33.]

Rav Kook's reference to Metushelaḥ etc. as pre-Abrahamic monotheists would appear to be derived from Rambam who wrote (Avodah Zarah 1:2):

> The Master of the Universe was only recognized by individuals in the world, such as Ḥanokh, Metushelaḥ, Noaḥ, Shem and Ever…

[28] Op. cit., 32.

APPENDIX I

Gender Universalism

The same verses that serve as our basis for the principles we have entitled "quantitative election" and the "sanctity of *mitzvot*," are juxtaposed by R. Moshe Feinstein in a 1976 responsum on the enduring question of women's *halakhic* rights:[29]

> One should also know that [the *halakhic* distinction of women] is not on account of an inferior status of *kedushah* from that of men, for in respect of *kedushah* they are equal to men with regard to their obligation towards *mitzvot*, which only depends upon the [essential] *kedushah* of a Jew, on account of which we were commanded in their performance. Furthermore, women, too, were included in all the verses that stipulate *kedushah* including that which is a prerequisite to the acceptance of Torah: "Be my treasure among the peoples… You shall then be unto me [a kingdom of priests and] a special nation." Those verses were addressed to "the house of Yaakov", which designates the women, and "told to the children of Israel," who are the men. Similarly: "You shall be people of sanctity unto Me," in the *sidrah* of Mishpatim (Shemot 22:30), "You shall be sacred" in the *sidrah* of *Kedoshim* (Vayikra 20:7), "For you are a sacred people unto the Lord your God" in the *sidrah* of *Re-eh* (Devarim14:2). Wherever one finds a reference to the sanctity of Is-

[29] *Iggerot Moshe*, Oraḥ Ḥayyim 4:49. While upholding the essential equality of men and women, he was adamantly opposed to any alterations in *halakhah*. It was partially in response to his strictures (along with those of Rabbi Joseph B. Soloveitchik) that Orthodox women agreed to constitute themselves as "prayer" or Tefillah groups, rather than as a minyan, or quorum. For a thorough discussion of this issue, see Dov Frimer & Aryeh Frimer: "Women's Prayer Services - Theory and Practice," Tradition, 32:2 (Spring 1998), pp. 5-118.

rael, it is addressed to women, too. Therefore, women, too, recite the formula of "Who has sanctified us with His *mitzvot*" when performing a *mitzvah*, just as men do, even on *mitzvot* the Torah does not obligate them to perform.

Rather, it is a leniency on the part of God, for whatever reason, to ease things for women (as discussed above) and not, forbid, on account of their inferiority. Moreover, in regard to the mutual responsibilities between husbands and wives, there is no distinction between his obligation towards her and hers towards him. Many women were prophetesses and had all the *halakhic* prerogatives of male prophets and in many respects they were praised by Scripture and by the Sages even more than the men. There is no disrespect shown to them by their exemption from Torah study and time-bound *mitzvot*, and they have no cause for protest...

APPENDIX II

"Loving All:" A Poem by Rav Kook[30]

I love everything.
I cannot keep from loving all beings,
all peoples.
In the depths of my heart
I wish for the splendor of all,
the mending of all.
My love for Israel is more fervent,
more profound,
but the inner longing
expands in its
power of love
over all, literally all.

---

[30] *Arpelei Tohar*, p. 31.

Communication: The basic building block of relationships with children and adolescents

David Pelcovitz

This paper will focus on three factors impacting on communication between parents and children, with substantive implications for educators.

The time factor

It is a popular belief that the current generation is far busier than previous ones. Recent literature suggests that, in fact, this may not be the case at all. Yet, surprisingly, what may be significant is not the fact of being busier but the perception that we indeed are.

Rosetto, Pennsylvania was the subject of a fascinating study. Beginning in the 1950's, medical researchers discovered unusual longevity among its citizens. Medical epidemiologists became interested in Rosetto when they discovered that the residents of this western Pennsylvania town were living far longer lives then those of their counterparts in similar Pennsylvania towns. In an attempt to better understand the process protecting the health of the residents of Rosetto the medical researchers compared the health habits – including dietary and exercise patterns – of Rosetto to those of surrounding towns, and found that those of Rosetto were no better – if anything, even worse – than those of their neighbors. With the mystery intensifying, and no apparent medical explanation, they moved into the town to observe the lifestyle. Their findings were startling.

Rosetto was settled in the 1880's almost entirely by immigrants from a small town in southern Italy, who brought with them a deep sense of community and cohesiveness. This sense of mutual commitment became an integral part of Rosetto's culture. Their sense of family extended far beyond that of the narrowly defined nuclear family. They were nosy; they were busybodies; they would sit on the front porch, and if a child was cutting school they would communicate that to the parents and school authorities. The town's residents placed tremendous emphasis on religious values and volunteering for the community. All this was absent in neighboring communities.

Starting in the 1980's there was a marked societal shift, not uncommon on the East Coast. The new generation of Rosetto had become acculturated to mainstream American norms, and in raising their children began to reject the southern Italian folkways. In 2005, the highest death rate in eastern Pennsylvania was recorded in Rosetto.[1] The implications regarding the impact of social networks on physical health are clear.

Allow me a personal reflection. When my wife was unable to join me in my own travels to conferences and conventions I would take along one of my children. We would spend some time together for a few days; s/he would help me set up my slides or posters. It was before the days of cell phones, and it became an opportunity to spend some unstructured quality time together. Although at the time it was not a conscious agenda, I noticed that it was during those trips that new lines of communication were opened. When I think back, it was during those trips that I had the deepest conversations with my children. Those were moments otherwise unavailable in the hurried routine of daily life.

To put a Jewish spin on this, there's a beautiful thought from Menaḥem Mendel of Kotzk. Chapter 127 of Tehillim is connected to child rearing and education, and verse 4 reads: "Like arrows in the hand of a warrior are sons …" Explaining the link between childrearing and an archer, the Kotzker Rebbe suggests that just as with an archer, the closer he draws the bow to his heart the further and straighter the arrow flies, so too with raising children; the closer we hold them to our heart, the further and straighter they go. The bottom line is that contemporary society generates a feeling of being harried, whether true or not, and it is that feeling which creates an impediment to our ability to communicate.

---

1 J.G. Bruhn and S. Wolf, *The Rosetto Story: An Anatomy of Health* (Norman, Okla.: University of Oklahoma Press, 1979); S. Wolf and J. G. Bruhn, *The Power of Clan: The Influence of Human Relationships on Heart Disease,* (New Brunswick, N.J.: Transaction Publishers, 1993); B. Egolf, J. Lasker, S. Wolf, L. Potvin, "The Rosetto Effect: a Fifty Year Comparison of Mortality Rates," *American Journal of Epidemiology* 125, no. 6 (1992): 1089-1092.

In the late 19th and early 20th centuries, hysterical paralysis was a common cause of referral to psychological professionals. Today there are very few documented cases of hysterical paralysis, that illness has apparently been replaced by chronic fatigue syndrome.[2] Sociologically speaking, we've moved from paralysis to fatigue; we are feeling tired and harried, and we are too close to it to see it clearly.

Harvard University's Kennedy School of Government gives a social capital score to every state of the union. Some states have high social capital scores, marked by indicators such as volunteerism, community service, caring for other people – what Jews would call a sense of *kehillah*. Other states are more focused on individuality, independence and self fulfillment, emphasizing the individual's personal and financial growth. Those studies have found that if you move from a low social capital state to a high social capital state, that is, if you move from a state where people aren't very caring and there isn't very much volunteer work to a state that has a more integrated sense of community along with a recognition that members of that community have an obligation to care for each other, it is as predictive of your health as whether or not you give up smoking. Joining one social group cuts your odds of dying over the next year in half; joining two groups cuts it by three quarters.[3]

The National Center on Addiction and Substance Abuse (CASA) at Columbia University has been conducting studies which have recently received significant attention. The survey of teens found that "the number of teens who have regular family dinners drops by 50 percent as their substance abuse risk increases sevenfold." The survey further demonstrates the importance of regular family dinners, finding that, "compared to teens who have family dinners twice a week or less, teens who have dinner with their families five or more nights in a week are 32 percent likelier never to have tried cigarettes, 45 percent likelier never to have tried alcohol, and 24 percent likelier never to have smoked pot."[4]

---

[2] van der Kolk, B., Pelcovitz, D., Roth, S., Mandel, F., McFarlane, A., Herman, J. (1996). "Dissociation, affect dysregulation and somatization: the complex nature of adaptation to trauma," *American Journal of Psychiatry* 153(Suppl), 83-93.

[3] http://www.ksg.harvard.edu/saguaro/factoids.htm

[4] http://www.casacolumbia.org/supportcasa/item.asp?cID=12&PID=86

What emerges as a recurring theme is that the investment of spending positive time with children has a profound effect on communication with parents and with child development. There is an emerging literature of longitudinal studies, following individuals from early childhood into young adulthood, looking at predictors of empathy in children. One major predictor found in each of those longitudinal studies is the amount of time parents spend with their children – the more time spent with children, the greater the likelihood that they will develop empathetic dispositions.

In today's society it is becoming increasingly difficult to facilitate the process in which parents prioritize spending time. Educators can play a significant role – facilitating parental awareness through parenting workshops and seminars which help parents understand the importance of creating time to spend with their children, so that the children know and feel that they are their parents' primary priority regardless of how busy the parents may be. There are a variety of rituals, and not only those built into the Jewish calendar, which can be incorporated into daily life which can accomplish this. These range from bedtime rituals to shopping trips to assignment of chores to family vacations. In the New York area there's an alarming trend in the right-wing day schools that the winter and spring vacations are intentionally scheduled at different times for the boys' and the girls' schools, so as to avoid social mixing. One net result of this is that families can no longer take vacations together, with a corresponding corrosive effect on parent-child and family dynamics – dynamics which, according to the research, are enormously predictive of stability, routine and the connectedness which emerges from the Kotzker's "holding our children close to our hearts."

I recently met a young girl whose father was a partner in a law firm. He had been very busy at work and felt guilty taking time off work to spend with her. One Sunday he took his daughter to the park, but during their entire time together his cell phone kept ringing. After a few hours she turned to him and said: "Daddy, you have to do me a favor and go back to the office. I'm used to not having you with me, and today I thought I would have you with me. But when you're on and off again like that and I think I have you but then you are pulled back, I just prefer not to have it at all." I've been hearing from some younger children that they have teachers who take calls during class when they think no administrators are looking. I've even had psychotherapy sessions in my office in which people were talking about the most intimate details of their lives, affairs that their spouse might be having, seriously considering divorce, worrying about a dying parent – which they interrupt to answer calls on their cell phones. An almost compulsive need to remain connected to work at all times has led to a corresponding loss of connection to what should be our most precious priority – our children.

Communication through modeling

Subtle messages indirectly communicated to children are often much more pervasive and powerful than direct education and teaching. The way adults act is far more profoundly influential on what children learn than what they say. What message is conveyed when parents lie about their child's age so that they can get them into a movie or Disney World at half price? Conversely, what do children learn from the adult who shows no consideration for the waiting taxi driver or is a rude to a waiter in a restaurant?

A memory burned in my mind dates back to my college days. Spending my painstakingly earned savings and with help from my parents, I bought a used car. I didn't know much about cars other than that they needed gas. One day it wouldn't start – I probably never changed the oil and the engine must have burned out. After placing an ad in the local newspaper we sold the car to an Irish man who knew a great deal about cars; he saw a good deal and gave us a $100 check for the car. On the following day, the man's irate wife rang our doorbell shouting anti-Semitic slurs, accusing us of cheating them, selling them a non-working vehicle. We had been straightforward about the car's condition, and it was probably a good deal for some one who knew how to fix cars. I was quite upset at the way she verbally attacked and accused us, and certainly had no intention of returning her money. As my father calmly listened to her, he took the check out of his pocket and tore it up, apologizing for her troubles. And if I remember correctly we let them keep the car.

Thinking back to all the years I studied in yeshiva and after that in graduate school, all the classes I heard and the studying of *mussar* and the sections of *Shulḥan Arukh* dealing with monetary matters, subconsciously, that one image of that scene with my father shaped my approach to money and to the sense of straightforwardness more than any formal educational program. Why? Because it was processed differently – in a way that speaks to a boy what communication is really about. And what communication is really about is all that right-hemisphere learning – non verbal education that is indirectly absorbed by modeling ourselves after those who we admire. As a number of my students have pointed out, the most valuable lessons they learned from admired teachers was observing the way they treated their wives and children as observed on a shabbaton spent at a *rebbe's* house.

In a published eulogy, Rabbi Soloveitchik describes what he learned from his mother.

> I used to have long conversations with my mother. In fact, it was a monologue rather then a dialogue. She talked and I "happened" to overhear. What did she talk about? I must use an *halakhic* term in order to answer this question: she talked about *me-inyana de-yoma* (ed. – the issues of the day, usually related to the Jewish calendar). I used to watch her arranging the house in honor of a holiday. I used to see her recite prayers; I used watch her recite the sidra every Friday night and I still remember the nostalgic tune. I learned from her very much.
>
> Most of all I learned that Judaism expresses itself not only in formal compliance with the law but also in a living experience. She taught me there is a flavor, a scent, a warmth to *mitzvot.* I learned from her the most important thing in life – the presence of the Almighty and the gentle pressure of His hand resting upon my frail shoulders.[5]

Rabbi Soloveitchik's language is the language of the right hemisphere, of the non verbal. This is the most potent form of communication.

---

[5] Rabbi Joseph B. Soloveitchik, "A Tribute to the Rebbitzen of Talne," *Tradition* 17:2 (Spring 1978) pp. 73-83

Communicating through acceptance

I'd like next to address communicating through acceptance. Much communication is done silently through the ways that teachers treat children; do they treat them in a way that shows patience and concern or that shows impatience and dismissiveness. At-risk students in the Orthodox community will often articulate that their break with the Orthodox community was triggered by a dismissive or disrespectful comment by a teacher. One student remarked that his Rabbi, commenting on a small suede *yarmulke* he was wearing, cynically told him that, "if you're going to wear a *yarmulke* like that you might as well go to McDonald's and eat a cheeseburger." The student's response was to remove the *yarmulke* and proceed to McDonald's to enjoy that cheeseburger. While the student's response clearly indicates that he had been struggling for a while, and the Rabbi's comment was not the sole cause of his rejection of Jewish life, had the Rabbi made a welcoming and embracing comment rather than a distancing and repelling one, the student could have been drawn back in.

In the same longitudinal studies cited earlier regarding the predictors of empathy in children another finding emerges. These studies find that it's not just the time spent in discussions around the dinner table, but the tenor of those discussions that play a significant role in communicating proper values to our children. Families in which parents show respect for the perspective of others, including the children, even as they disagree, are more likely to effectively communicate to their children the value of empathically relating to others. It is easy to imagine a Friday night table at which the parents complain bitterly that the principal of the school or a teacher did something wrong. If the children overhear the tone of disparagement and cynicism then they will learn exactly those messages. If, however, the adults at the table can set a tone that communicates that even though there is disagreement, it can be experienced while showing respect for the other position, perhaps even the attempt to see the issue through the eyes of the other (while still maintaining the right to disagree), then that can help develop empathy.

Interestingly, the ability to respect the perspective of others is one of the key predictors of success in general, and in the ability to succeed in a good marriage. John Mordechai Gottman, one of the leading marital therapy researchers in the world, connects people to biofeedback equipment and carefully studies couples as they fight. Within seven minutes, he can predict with 94% accuracy whether that couple will be divorced within five years. It's not an elusive science – his main point is that it's all about communication style. Marriages and parent-child relationships are most likely to thrive if we communicate with our children and spouses in a manner which shows a healthy respect for their perspective, and in a manner that accepts them for who they are.

There is interesting research on communication styles in facing pain and illness. Children (and adults) have a variety of coping mechanisms, for dealing with stressful experiences such as painful medical treatment.

On one pole of the continuum is the individual who does not want any information on the nature or details of their treatment. This type, which the literature either calls a "distracter" or "blunter"[6], would rather focus on anything else other than their illness or the medical care. For the distracter, hospitals need to provide distractions such as books, videos or computer games. The patient will engross himself in the distraction of his choice as the medical procedure, no matter how painful, is being performed, and their experience of discomfort will be significantly reduced as the child creates for himself a hypnotic or trancelike engagement in the activity.

On the other pole is the "attender" who needs to constantly monitor, process and discuss the stressful situation. Such individuals want to know every detail of their illness and treatment. They ask doctors for second opinions, research their condition on their own and offer to help the doctor when they need to undergo a painful procedure. The research demonstrates that "forcing" medical information on a distracter or pushing distracting material on an attender will actually worsen their condition and intensify their discomfort.

This research is already echoed in the Talmud (Yoma 75a) in a debate between R. Ami and R. Asi. Commenting on a difficult word (*yash-ḥena*) in Mishlei 12:25, one explains that it suggests that an in-

6 Miller, S. M., Fang, C. Y., Diefenbach, M. A., Bales, C. B., "Tailoring psychosocial interventions to the individual's health information-processing style," In Baum, A. and Andersen, B. (Eds.) *Psychosocial Interventions for Cancer* (American Psychological Association Press, Washington, D.C., 2001):343-362.

dividual with worries should distract himself to remove them (reading the difficult word as *yis-ḥena*) from his mind, while the other suggests that the worried individual should talk it out (as in, *yesiḥena*) to calm himself. Essentially, both positions are valid for different personality types. This same notion is true for the rest of the people in our intimate interactions; we must learn and respect the individual communication styles of our family members.

I recall being at the first Chai Lifeline retreat nearly fifteen years ago. The first person I met was a man who accosted me. He angrily asserted that he did not want to be at the retreat and was forced to be there by his wife. He was a medical doctor with a son suffering from leukemia. He explained that his method of coping was to focus on obtaining the finest medical care available for the treatment of his son. He did not believe in the efficacy of psychological support; and was tired of "talking about" his feelings regarding his son's illness. Much to his wife's consternation, I calmly suggested that he return to his hotel room to relax. I did not see him for the rest of the weekend.

Seven years later, at a weekend for at-risk adolescents in the Orthodox community, I saw the same couple again. Sensing my apprehension as he approached, he reassured me that I would not be subject to another angry tirade. He explained that after his son recovered from his illness, his older daughter began to express that she had felt neglected during the time they were preoccupied with the cancer, and started to act out in serious ways. This time, when his wife asked him to attend a seminar in which they would "talk out" the problems, he went willingly. The turning point in their marriage came on the heels of the first crisis. At that time his wife was pushing him in one direction while he was pushing in the other. Now, they had both come to accept that there are different communication and coping styles, and that those needed to be mutually accepted and respected.

Fundamentally, when people know that they are accepted and loved, they can feel secure enough in themselves and their position to be open to other opinions, and perhaps even to change. This is true for adults, and all the more so for children.

Students Encountering the Media and the Internet: A scientific analysis amongst youth in the Jewish community

Scott J. Goldberg

In recent years there has been an unfortunate increase in the number of adolescents from Orthodox families who have been seriously disruptive, rebellious and defiant.[1] While there is uncertainty about why this phenomenon is more prevalent today, some speculate that parents of this generation having greater difficulty setting limits, the yeshiva education system is placing greater demands for learning on all children yet is not very tolerant of children who do not fit into the mold, and there are more profound external influences through media exposure.

Risk Factors

Current understanding of the etiology of antisocial behavior in the Orthodox Jewish community comes from a combination of the general psychological literature on antisocial behavior,[2] as well as from a limited number of studies conducted specifically in the Orthodox Jewish community. In a survey of twenty-five organizations dealing with this population including schools, hotlines, and mental health professionals in Brooklyn's Orthodox Jewish community, Danziger[3] found 6.6% of adolescents to be "at-risk." This amounts to approxi-

---

1 See Russell, S., & Blumenthal, N., *Children in Crisis: Detection and intervention* (Teaneck, NJ: Nefesh, 2000); Pelcovitz, D. "The At-Risk Orthodox Jewish Adolescent," in *Azrieli Papers* (NY: Azrieli Graduate School of Jewish Education and Administration, 2005); Danziger, Y., *The incidence of at-risk youth in the Orthodox Jewish community of Brooklyn, NY,* Report to the New York City Department of Youth and Community Development, Metropolitan Council on Jewish Poverty (1999).

2 Rutter, M., "Psychosocial influences: Critiques, findings, and research needs," *Development and Psychopathology*, 12 (2000): 375 – 405.

3 See note 1.

mately 1500 teens engaging in "serious at-risk behavior." These same organizations were shocked by what was considered an underestimate of the problem, with an additional 11 – 12% (approximately 2500) of adolescents believed to be "at-risk".[4] Further one may question the term "at-risk" for this population, as most teens who are labeled in this way are already exhibiting major behavior problems. This, of course, leaves untreated a sizable group of children who are truly "at-risk" for the development of problems in the future.

Russell & Blumenthal,[5] providing the perspective of Orthodox Jewish mental health professionals, educators, and community leaders, identified various child risk factors, family risk factors, and environmental risk factors for antisocial behavior. Child risk factors include the dysregulated child (e.g., hyperactive), the depressed or anxious child, and the child who feels like a failure because of learning or social problems. Family risk factors entail poor parenting/marriage issues and membership in a reconstructed family. Environmental risk factors involve abuse and stress.

In the general psychological literature, Rutter[6] provides slightly different categories of risk: familial, social, and learning issues. A meta-analysis by Serketich and Dumas found that the effect size for parenting intervention is eighty-six percent.[7] This is not to suggest that we blame parents for a child's behavior problem. However, a parenting style characterized by punishment, inconsistency, neglect, and emotionalism places a child at increased risk for antisocial behavior.[8] In the Orthodox Jewish community specifically, Feldman found that a disciplinary approach characterized by a balance between appropri-

---

[4] See note 1.

[5] See note 1.

[6] See note 2.

[7] Serketich, W., & Dumas, J., "The effectiveness of behavioural parent-training to modify antisocial behaviour in children," *Behaviour Therapy*, 27(1996): 171 – 186.

[8] Loeber, R., & Hay, D., "Key issues in the development of aggression and violence from childhood to early adulthood," *Annual Review of Psychology*, 48 (1997): 371 – 410; Kilgore, K., Snyder, J., & Lentz, C., "The contribution of parental discipline, parental monitoring, and school risk to early-onset conduct problems in African American boys and girls," *Developmental Psychology*, 36 (2000): 835 – 845.

ate limits and sufficient love and caring may be a protective factor against behavior problems.[9]

Concerning social functioning, feelings of isolation from a community appear to cause aggression.[10] Although it sounds intuitive that social connectedness will engender positive behavior, with whom one is connected is important, as seen in the Cambridge-Somerville Youth Study. Antisocial youth were provided with a summer camp "intervention" including what was considered the best possible care at the time. These youth were followed for 30 years after this intervention and were found to have experienced more school dropout, incarceration, and early death (compared to a comparison group that did not have the summer camp "intervention").[11] Such effects were explained as a result of deviancy training that occurred during the camp – the children taught each other how to act antisocial. Today, with the level of media exposure of our youth, they may be experiencing similar deviancy training beyond the direct exposure to other antisocial youth.

The role of language-based learning disabilities in relation to behavior problems was explored by Tomblin, Zhang, Buckwalter, and Catts.[12] While they found that reading disability mediates the relationship between language impairment and behavior problems, the role that social cohesion plays in this relationship was not explored explicitly. Indeed, rather than consider these as entirely separate factors, one may consider them interconnected and interdependent based on

---

[9] Feldman, A., *Parenting style and behaviors associated with ADHD in at-risk adolescents in the Orthodox Jewish community*, Unpublished doctoral dissertation, Georgia State University, College of Education, Department of Counseling and Psychological Services (2004).

[10] Twenge, J. M., Baumeister, R. F., Tice, D. M., & Stucke, T. S., "If you can't join them, beat them: Effects of social exclusion on aggressive behavior," *Journal of Personality and Social Psychology*, 81, 6 (2001): 1058 – 1069.

[11] Powers, E., & Witmer, H., *An experiment in the prevention of delinquency: The Cambridge-Somerville Youth Study*, (New York: Columbia University Press, 1951).

[12] Tomblin, J. B., Zhang, X., Buckwalter, P., & Catts, H., "The association of reading disability, behavioral disorders, and language impairment among second-grade children," *Journal of Child Psychology and Psychiatry and Allied Disciplines*, 41, 4(2000): 473 – 482.

Bronfenbrenner's ecological theory of development.[13] Bronfenbrenner suggests that one can only understand the experiences of an individual through the interaction between the individual and multiple contexts. That is, the child is affected not only by his/her individual system of development, but also by the people and situations with whom an individual comes in contact on a daily basis (e.g., family, school, etc.), various settings which exert control over the child's life but of which the child lacks any membership or control (e.g., a school board), and the shared culture and values of the community in which the child lives. Each of these domains may affect a child's behavior and define how that behavior should be understood and evaluated. In the only empirical study that considered the interplay between risk factors for antisocial behavior in the Orthodox Jewish community, Goldberg[14] found that the commonly accepted categories of risk factors for anti-social behavior in the general population, namely family, social, and learning problems[15] manifest themselves differently in the Orthodox Jewish community as two risk factors: family and social, with learning problems being one path to the social problems.

The specific effect of media exposure, including Internet use and television viewing, has not been explored in relation to various risk factors for problem behaviors. Of course, media exposure may complicate the above model by bringing contexts further away from the child, into the child's more immediate spheres of influence. Further, media exposure may affect each of the domains of risk, family, social, and learning, in unique ways. This paper will present the results of a pilot study that considered the role of media exposure as a contributing factor to the phenomenon of antisocial behavior amongst teens in the Orthodox Jewish community.

---

13 Bronfenbrenner, U. *The ecology of human development: Experiments by nature and design* (Cambridge, MA: Harvard University Press, 1979).

14 Goldberg, S. J., The relationship between English (L1) and Hebrew (L2) reading and externalizing behavior amongst Orthodox Jewish boys, Ph.D. dissertation, New York University. (2004).

15 Rutter, op. cit.

Media Effects on Family, Socialization, and Learning

Television

Studies concerning the effect of television on social behavior have yielded somewhat mixed results. The following represents a sampling of the research in the field. While negative effects of media use will comprise the majority of the remainder of this review, one cannot ignore the "no problem" studies that have been conducted. For example, contrary to the expectations of many, the introduction of television to the island of St. Helene resulted in no change in social behavior.[16] Of course, that study or others of its kind do not paint the whole picture of the effects of media exposure. Indeed, how can one explain the following effects? In South Africa there was more than a doubling of the murder rate in the first generation of TV watchers. One-quarter of WWII soldiers were unable to kill the first time they were in a situation that necessitated it compared with soldiers in Vietnam combat who had no such difficulty. Other countries are censoring the children's television programming of the United States because of high violent content.

Research on such negative effects abounds. Krcmar and Greene found that undesirable exposure to violence oftentimes lead to television induced aggression.[17] While this finding appears to substantiate the hyperbolic pleas of some religious leaders in the Jewish community to rid our homes of television, these *negative effects were a result of more than two hours of viewing per day.* The research is concerned with more than just violence. Television programs contain explicit sexual content, and have been found to shape young viewer's perceptions of teen pregnancies and unwed mothers.[18] Nathanson found that this

---

[16] Charlton, T., Gunter, B. and Hannan, A., *Broadcast Television Effects in a Remote Community*, Hillsdale, New Jersey: Lawrence Erlbaum (2000).

[17] Krcmar, M., & Greene, K., "Predicting exposure to and uses of violent television," *Journal of Communication*, 49(1999): 25-45.

[18] Larson, M. S., "Sex roles and soap operas: What adolescents learn about single motherhood," *Sex Roles*, 35 (1/2)(1996): 97-110.

has led to increased parental mediation, and that parental attitudes toward television have a significant effect on children's attitudes.[19]

Internet

Internet use has become pervasive and indispensable, opening up educational opportunities and vistas once only imagined. In a national sample of children and teenagers asked to choose which medium to bring with them to a desert isle, more children from 8 to 18 chose a computer with Internet access than any other medium.[20] Children spend a large amount of time using computers in the home. The Annenberg Survey found that children ages 2 to 17 in homes with computers spend 1 hour 37 minutes per day on computers.[21] Looking only at teens, the HomeNet study reports that teens with Internet access at home use the computer only 3 hours per week, less than the average found in the Annenberg study.[22] However, they also report that more than 10% of children use the computer more than 16 hours per week. While girls appear to subscribe to listservs more than boys, boys tend to use the Internet more than girls.

Like with behavior, there are studies that reveal positive effects of media use on academic abilities. For example, Schmar-Dobler found that by conducting searches on the Internet, students learn to focus on speed and efficiency when reading. Furthermore, students learn to scan text and locate key pivot words, an essential reading comprehension skill.[23] Additionally, high school grades do not seem to

---

[19] Nathanson, A.I., "Parent and child perspectives on the presence and meaning of parental television mediation," *Journal of Broadcasting and Electronic Media* 45(2001): 201-220.

[20] Rideout, V. J., Foehr, U. G., Roberts, D. F., & Brodie, M., *Kids and media @ the new millennium: A comprehensive analysis of children's media use.* Unpublished report, Kaiser Family Foundation, Menlo Park, CA. (1999).

[21] Stanger, J. D. & Gridina, N., *Media in the Home 1999: The Fourth Annual Survey of Parents and Children, Annenberg Public Policy Center Survey Series No. 5*, University of Pennsylvania. Public Policy Center (1999).

[22] Kraut, R., Lundmark, V., Patterson, M, Kiesler, S., Mukhopadhyay, T., & Scherlis, W., "Internet paradox: A social technology that reduces social involvement and psychological well-being?" *American Psychologist* 53(1998): 1017-1031.

[23] Schmar-Dobler, E., "Reading on the Internet: the Link Between Literacy and Technology," *Journal of Adolescent & Adult Literacy*, September

be negatively impacted by Internet use. In fact, high school grades appear to be positively correlated with Internet use.[24] The results of a 1998 Annenberg survey of parents suggested that Internet use had a positive effect by displacing television viewing.[25] However, Adoni found that media use did not result in a decrease in reading. That is, time on the Internet appears to decrease television viewing time but not reading time.[26] Turow[27] also concluded that 70% of parents in households with computers said that children can discover fascinating and useful things on Internet and that 60% of parents say children without Internet are "disadvantaged" compared with peers who have the Internet.

These studies showing positive or neutral effects do not paint the entire picture the effects of media use on academic achievement. Studies have shown that reading comprehension is negatively affected.[28] Not only do studies show that television viewing inhibits children's reading comprehension skills, but Blanton, Moorman, Hayes, and Warner suggests that Internet use, in fact, displaces studying and homework. Indeed, the number of students studying for less than an hour a week almost doubled in the last 15 years.[29]

2003.

[24] Sparks, G. G., "Developmental differences in children's reports of fear induced by the mass media," Child Study Journal, 16(1)(1986): 55-66; Rocheleau, B., "Computer use by school-aged children: trends, patterns, and predictors," *Journal of Educational Computing Research* 12(1)(1995): 1-17.

[25] Stanger, J., "Television in the Home 1998: The Third Annual Survey of Parents and Children." Survey Series No. 4, Philadelphia: University of Pennsylvania, Annenberg (1998); Turow, J. "The internet and family: The view from parents; The view from the press," Philadelphia, PA, Annenberg Public Policy Center:44 (1999). Annenberg Public Policy Center of the University of Pennsylvania, Report No. 27.

[26] Adoni, H., "Literacy and reading in a multimedia environment," *Journal of Communication*, 45 (1995): 152–174.

[27] See note 25.

[28] Koolstra, C.M., van der Voort, T.H.A., & van der Kamp, L.J.T., "Television's impact on children's reading comprehension and decoding skills: A 3-year panel study," *Reading Research Quarterly* 32(2)(1997): 128-52.

[29] Blanton, W. E., Moorman, G. B., Hayes, B. A., & Warner, M. W., "Effects of participation in the Fifth Dimension on far transfer," *Journal of Educational Computing Research* 16(1997): 371-396.

Social interactions appear to be affected negatively by computer use. In fact, solitude accompanies computer use and may be a result. More than 1/5 of children ages 8–18 have a computer in their bedroom, children report "electronic friendships" with the machine, and over sixty percent of computer time for junior and high school students is spent alone.[30] Frequent gamers meet friends outside of school more than less frequent gamers.[31] There appear to be no differences in the quality or intensity of these social interactions.[32] While peer interaction is negatively affected by computer time, family interactions do not appear to be impacted.[33]

Not only is social interaction itself affected, but the social well-being of the child is likewise at stake. The HomeNet study found that the more time spent online the greater declines in social and psychological well-being. Specifically, more Internet use is related to a decline in social involvement (communication within family and size of people's social networks), an increase in loneliness, and depression. Further, frequent users tend to be lonely, have deviant values, and have weak emotional/social skills.[34] Computer use is often seen as a displacement of social activities, a substitute of poorer quality social relationships for better ones.[35] Internet relationships tend to be weak tie relationships – that is, they provide less consequential social support and are weaker compared to "live" relationships. [36] While not always the case, Parks and Roberts found that online relationships

---

[30] Rideout, et al.

[31] Colwell J, Grady C, Rhaiti S., "Computer games, self-esteem and gratification of needs in adolescents," *Journal of Community and Applied Social Psychology* 5 (1995): 195–206.

[32] Phillips, C. A., Rolls, S., Rouse, A., & Griffiths, M. D., "Home video game playing in schoolchildren: a study of incidence and patterns of play," *Journal of Adolescence* 18(1995): 687-691.

[33] Mitchell, A.A., "Some issues surrounding research on the effects of 'feeling advertisements,'" *Advances in Consumer Research* 13(1985): 623-28.

[34] Engelberg, E., & Sjöberg, L., "Internet use, social skills and adjustment," *CyberPsychology & Behavio*r 7(2004): 41-48.

[35] Krackhardt, D., "The strength of strong ties," in N. Nohria & R. Eccles (Eds.), *Networks and organizations: Structure, form, and action* (Harvard Business School Press, 1994).

[36] Wellman, B., Salaff, J. Dimitrova, D., Garton, L., Gulia, M., & Haythornthwaite, C., "Computer networks as social networks: Collabora-

generally remain online.[37] This is especially important given the dangers of online relationships. Indeed, the Internet (unlike other previous forms of telecommunication) contains many popular applications (e.g., listservs, chat rooms, MUDs – multiuser dungeons, etc.) which *encourage* strangers to communicate.

Like the threshold of two hours of television discussed above, the effects of the Internet must also be tempered and understood in context. Studies suggest that there is a diminishing effect over time. Initially, the more hours someone uses the Internet per week the more their psychological and social well-being will decline. However, after twelve months smaller declines in psychological and social well-being are seen. Argote and Epple posit that early exposure has larger consequences, users learn to use the Internet more wisely, and the technology is changing (AIM, ICQ, etc.) to provide "Buddy lists," which increases the likelihood that communication will be with people one already knows.[38]

Studies of Internet use, like those on television viewing, show a connection between media consumption and violence. Parents who say that they oversee computer use may benefit from the research that suggests that children find ways of exposing themselves to these types of media. Research found that playing violent video games even for a short period of time (short-term exposure) led to increased aggression.[39] Further, in a survey of Internet/computer game knowledge 80% of children surveyed knew *Duke Nukem* (a violent video game) but only 5% of parents knew the game. Perhaps most compelling is the desensitization that occurs with the playing of violent games on

---

tive work, telework, and virtual community," *Annual Review of Sociology* 22(1996): 213-238. Also Kraut, et al.

37 Parks, M. R. & Roberts, L.D., "Making MOOsic: The development of personal relationships on-line and a comparison to their off-line counterparts," http://psych.curtin.edu.au/people/robertsl/moosic.htm (1997)

38 Argote, L. and Epple, D., "Learning curves in manufacturing," *Science* 247(1990), 920–924.

39 Cooper, J. & Mackie, D., "Video games and aggression in children," *Journal of Applied Social Psychology* 16(1986): 726-744; Irwin, A.R. and Gross, A.M., "Cognitive tempo, violent video games, and aggressive behavior in young boys," *Journal of Family Violence* 10, 337-350; Johnson, J.G. et al. (2002) "Television viewing and aggressive behaviour during adolescence and adulthood," *Science*, 295(1995): 2468-2471.

the computer.[40] Perhaps most disturbing is that the military uses these violent videogames to desensitize soldiers to kill.[41]

Parents, educators, and psychologists are not only concerned about violence and social well-being. Numerous concerns revolve around exposure to sexually explicit topics. Livingstone has found that children use the Internet to experiment with themes of sexuality and that many children who view upsetting content (including explicit sexual content) online fail to report it to their parents.[42]

As a result of this general information, Jewish parents have echoed the sentiments of parents, educators, and policymakers in the general population, who have serious concerns about the negative impact television viewing and Internet use may have on children.[43] In November, 2005, the Orthodox community in Lakewood, NJ banned the Internet. However, only speculation concerning the application of these studies has informed the discussion of such topics in the Jewish community. Thus, the choices that children, parents and schools in the Jewish community make concerning the level of exposure children will have to these forms of media may be based on inappropriately generalized information. This may lead to overzealousness or underzealousness on the part of the leaders of the Jewish community.

Pilot Study

The population for this pilot study was a group of 30 Orthodox Jewish university students who had attended Modern, Centrist, and Yeshiva Orthodox high schools.[44] The population included twenty-one (21) male students and nine (9) female students ranging in age from 18 to 28 (Mean Age = 21.63).

---

[40] Rule, B., & Ferguson, T., "The effects of media violence on attitudes, emotions and cognition," *Journal of Social Issues* 42(1986): 29-50.

[41] Platoni, K., "The Pentagon goes to the video arcade: Video games used as military training," *The Progressive* 63(1999): 27-30.

[42] Livingstone, S., "Children's use of the Internet: Reflections on the emerging research agenda," *New Media & Society* 5(2) (2003): 147–166.

[43] See Lawrence Keleman's *To Kindle A Soul* (Jerusalem: Targum/Leviathan, 2001).

[44] The classification of these schools is based on Schick, M., *A census of Jewish Day Schools in the United States* (New York, NY: Avi Chai Foundation, 2000).

Students were recruited on a university campus via posted advertisements for the study. Each student completed questionnaires individually that asked them to reflect back on their high school years in terms of religious practice, behavior, and media (television, Internet) use. The study proposed to answer questions on the relationship between these various areas. Results are organized based on the aforementioned areas of risk for antisocial behavior and mainly concentrated around social and learning factors.

Media Use and Socialization

As with the general population, television viewing was related to relaxation[45]. However, when one considers this finding in light of the findings of Krcmar and Greene, namely that negative effects are seen only when there is more than two hours of television watched per day the results are slightly different. Those who watch more than two hours of television per day[46] do not feel more relaxed than those who watch less than two hours of television per day,[47] at a statistically significant level.[48] The magnitude of this difference (effect size) was large.[49]

While Internet use was also related to relaxation,[50] it is of concern that it also related to a user's desire to be alone.[51] Concerning television use and socialization, the results depend on the type of show one is watching. While cartoons were likely to be watched with friends,[52] other shows were more affiliated with aloneness, boredom, and other problems. Those who watch dramas were likely to do so when bored,[53] when they wanted to be alone,[54] and they related to at least one char-

45 ($r = .473$, $p < .01$)
46 ($M=1.82$, $SD = .87$)
47 ($M=2.61$, $SD = .98$)
48 ($t(23) = 2.26, p<.05$)
49 (Eta Squared = .159 (15.9%))
50 ($r = .556$, $p<.01$)
51 ($r = .456$, $p<.05$)
52 ($r = .454$, $p<.05$)
53 ($r = .4$, $p<.05$)
54 ($r = .382$, $p<.05$)

acter.[55] For the latter, it may be that the characters are the viewer's social outlet. Sitcom viewers were likely to watch and then feel lonely.[56]

Perhaps the most disturbing finding relates to reality television. Those who watch reality television tended to relate to at least one character.[57] People reported that they have more energy after watching reality television[58] and feel more aggressive after watching a reality television show.[59]

Media Use and Academics

In the present study, television viewing was moderately and statistically significantly associated with increased achievement as measured by GPA.[60] Further, there was no indication of displacement of reading or other learning. However, hierarchical multiple regression (mediating analysis) showed that increased relaxation and discussions with peers moderates the relationship between television viewing and academic achievement. That is to say, of those who watch television, those who do not use television as a prosocial tool (to relax or to later discuss with peers), may not be successful academically.

Discussion

The Nefesh *Children in Crisis* manual delineates that the common thread that consistently runs through the narratives of children displaying antisocial behavior in the Orthodox Jewish community is feelings of alienation and exclusion. These youth find a connection with family and peers, and often have a history of academic failure.[61] Indeed, this parallels the risk factors discussed by Rutter in the general community.[62] Goldberg, studying these risk factors in the Orthodox Jewish community, concluded that for children in bilingual situations, the relation between reading and behavior may be a consequence of the social exclusion that results from children's inability to partake in

---

55 ($r = .596$, $p < .01$)
56 ($r = .512$, $p < .01$)
57 ($r = .553$, $p < .01$)
58 ($r = .582$, $p < .01$)
59 ($r = .421$, $p < .05$)
60 ($r = .421$, $p < .05$)
61 See note 1.
62 See note 2.

the literate activities of their culture.[63] Children in crisis consistently describe finding such feelings of belonging only when among similarly alienated friends.

It is within this context of alienation that the results of the current pilot study find particular meaning. When accompanied by a desire to be alone, Internet and television use was related to negative outcomes. Such negative outcomes included a correlation with aloneness and boredom. Reality television was related to the most negative results. Not only are those who watch reality television likely to relate to a character in the show, but the aggressive behavior classically associated with television viewing manifest itself in the present study only connected to reality television.

While the present study showed some positive relationship between media use and academic achievement, this relationship is dependent on the viewer relaxing when watching television or discussing the viewing with peers. That is to say, when a positive or prosocial purpose is associated with the television viewing, the positive relationship with academic achievement may be seen.

Of course, the results of the present study must be considered in light of several limitations including a small sample size and measurement of reflections on previous behaviors not current behaviors. Further study is needed to better understand the relationship between the risk factors for antisocial behavior in the Orthodox Jewish community and media use. Additionally, religious belief and behavior may be impacted and should therefore be examined. While the sample in the present study was too small for analysis, differences between boys and girls in terms of media use and the various behaviors discussed (e.g., aggression) should be explored. Given these limitations, the results are still thought provoking, a foundation on which to plan further research, and mostly consistent with previous findings in the general research literature.

No doubt, parents and educators can play an important role in mediating the effects of media exposure. The results of the present study, in the context of the research that precedes it, suggest that television and Internet use should be connected to social functioning for children. Television and computers should not become a babysitter for even a short period of time and certainly not for several hours

[63] See note 14.

a day. Rather, parents and educators should utilize these powerful tools to help youth relax, connect with peers, and to increase academic achievement. Facilitating discussions between youth on topics viewed on television and the Internet is important. Parents and educators should talk with children about the shows watched and the sites visited in order to provide greater context and meaning for the children. Without such filtering, television and Internet use promise to provide our children with an education inconsistent with the values of our homes and schools.

II. From Modernity to Post-Modernity

Perspectives for the Future of Jewish Education

David J. Schnall

Arthur Hertzberg is quoted as saying that Jews are a people who can't take yes for an answer. Even when things go well, we often have difficulty simply accepting that, and instead focus on problems, obstacles and premonitions. In that context, it is important that we begin by celebrating the impressive accomplishments of North American Jewish education over the recent decades and in particular, three constituencies who have contributed to that success.

First are the parents who send their children to Jewish day schools. Contemporary Americans have endless ways by which to expend disposable income, and in this profoundly material society there is a constantly expanding range of options to invest in oneself or one's financial future. American Jews, however, in ever growing numbers, are choosing to invest in the future of their children and in the future of the Jewish community, through formal and informal Jewish education.

This is especially noteworthy in light of the very substantial costs involved and the frequent dearth of financial or even moral support. Far too rarely do we celebrate parents and grandparents who have chosen to delay their own material gratification in lieu of an investment in their children and in the future of the Jewish community. As practitioners and academics, it behooves us to take pause and to acknowledge this sacrifice and achievement. By most estimates, the current day school population numbers over 200,000, and while there is much potential for still greater growth, this represents about one hundred percent increase over the past twenty five years, even as the general population of the American Jewish community has fallen during that same period. To parents and grandparents, we must extend our thanks.

At the same time, we spend too little time celebrating the Jewish educators, who often must delay not only personal, material gratification (probably to a far greater extent than most parents) but professional gratification, as well. I am confident that most Jewish educators could have pursued successful careers in other professions which offer greater material benefits and upward mobility, both personally and professionally.

The sacrifices they make, whether financially or in terms of status and prestige, are rarely acknowledged properly. Sadly, the self-same parents who sacrifice to send their children to day schools often discourage those children from pursuing a career in Jewish education. As a community, it is incumbent upon us to reward those who choose to pursue this noble calling: financial remuneration, fringe benefits, health insurance, and a host of other compensations that are commonplace in virtually every other field. Most important of all, we must extend to them the social and communal status that befits those who have chosen to facilitate the single most important factor ensuring the health and future of Jewish tradition and continuity.

The third group I applaud here are the students themselves. Here too, our general culture provides numerous mechanisms with which young people may spend the extra time that they invest attending in Jewish schools. Sociologists and demographers offer painful assessments regarding our general youth culture, with repeated studies concluding that contemporary Jewish youth are narcissistic and self-absorbed, wrapped up in rock music and electronic gadgetry. They show precious little interest in the values and traditions of their people as they follow a one-way trip to spiritual oblivion. It remains for these 200,000 day school students to prove us all wrong, to turn these data on their head and reclaim their distinction as tomorrow's Jewish leaders. There is little doubt that the very soul of Jewish life will largely be determined in the classroom. It behooves us to applaud those that have chosen to fight the trend. Far too rarely do we acknowledge just how important they are and how much depends upon them.

The 2000-01 Jewish Population Survey

Let us move from the celebratory comments to some data driven observations based on preliminary assessments of the year 2000-01 Jewish population survey.[1] Steven Cohen has already reaffirmed that intensive Jewish education, defined as day school education for a minimum of 7-9 years (estimated at 6000-8000 hours), is a profoundly

---

[1] The survey can be viewed at http://www.ujc.org/content_display.html?ArticleID=60346

important variable in basic continuity and affiliation into the next generation. Based on the year 2000 survey, Cohen demonstrates that day school education accounts for a 20% increase in Jewish identification among the current adult generation of American Jews more than any other single variable.

Interestingly, the second most important variable is the number of years of attendance in a Jewish camp, with 5-6 years being the critical number. This raises some important questions about the line we have arbitrarily drawn between formal and informal Jewish education, both in the schools and camp settings, and perhaps, most importantly, in the community at large. We may be making a mistake by overemphasizing the differences and reinforcing the limitations and restrictions that divide formal and informal education, the affective versus the cognitive as they impact upon the behavioral. Our mandate is to integrate both, and the combination of the two creates the context for a more effective educational program.

I would like to focus on another facet of this study which has not as yet been highlighted. The data suggest that approximately one third of the survey respondents have not had any exposure whatsoever to Jewish education – neither formal nor informal – and those numbers are virtually identical for the group under the age of forty and those over the age of forty. Despite the increase in day school enrollment, there is a substantial hard core of the Jewish population which is untouched by any of our efforts. In fact, the increase in day school enrollment has in large measure come at the expense of Hebrew school enrollment, so that while the level of the Jewish education received by participants may be intensifying, the total participation in basic exposure to Jewish education remains constant. Projecting toward the future, there is no reason to believe that the "unmoved" part of the adult Jewish population will change substantively.

The statistics also reveal a very substantial dropout rate from the elementary schools to the high schools. While the day schools have a fairly high rate of retention (that is, their graduates continue in Jewish high schools), for the Hebrew school, supplementary school and congregational school, the retention rate drops precipitously. The result is that approximately two-thirds of adults over the age of forty have no Jewish education beyond seventh grade. In stark contrast, those under forty are five times more likely to have continued their Jewish education beyond the elementary school level, in good measure because they were more likely to attend a Jewish day schools whose retention rate is that much higher.

Women's education

Perhaps even more stark are the corresponding data for women under the age of forty. For an example, female respondents under age forty are approximately four times more likely to have attended an elementary Jewish day school than have their mothers or older sisters. Similarly, women under the age of forty are five times more likely to have had high school level day school education than their mothers or older sisters.

Put simply, the current generation of younger Jewish women has a level of Jewish education and literacy unprecedented in its depth, breadth and intensity. Women are increasingly engaged in Jewish learning, full-time and part-time, and have greater access to serious Jewish study than at any point in our history.

If I may add a fourth cause for celebration in the success of day school education it is in this area: the expansive Jewish education for young women, particularly, though by no means exclusively, in the Orthodox community. Yet the celebration raises numerous questions. How will these young women employ their Jewish skills and competencies? What provisions will the community make to recognize and exploit this unprecedented cadre of knowledgeable, educated women? What positions of leadership will be available to them, both within Jewish education as well as within the community at large? Will the community as a whole, including its Orthodox and *haredi* elements, be prepared to restructure itself to make room for an educated, female leadership role? How will Jewish men deal with marital partners who may be more knowledgeable than they? Even *brakhot* bring challenges.[2]

---

[2] A comment on women's learning. It is fascinating, and somewhat distressing, to observe the expansion of Talmudic and quasi-Talmudic studies for women (the latter among those ideologically opposed to women studying Talmud). Whichever position one takes on this knotty issue, a word about teaching method is in order. I am convinced that the way we teach Talmud to young men is fundamentally flawed. Talmud study for women represents

Education of the Jewish immigrant population

Still another important finding that emerges from the JPS data relates to the notable number of foreign-born respondents. Projections suggest a growing proportion of emigrants from Eastern Europe, Israel and parts of the Mid-East – primarily Iran, Iraq, Morocco and Syria. Nearly half have had no exposure to Jewish education whatsoever.[3] Yet among the cohort of these immigrants under age forty, we also find that approximately 30% have had full time intensive day school education, with about equal propensity among women as among men. Quite distinct from the American-born population, where there is a continuum of educational exposure, in the immigrant group there is a dramatic gap between those who have had an intensive Jewish education and those who have virtually none. Most likely, this is because Hebrew schools and supplementary schools are a uniquely Western phenomenon virtually unknown in Eastern Europe, the Arab world, and in Israeli Jewish education.

Addressing the needs of this population may represent a unique opportunity, indeed a renaissance for supplementary and congregational schools. This population may not be prepared to send their children to day schools and may lack the financial means as well. Yet they may be prepared to have them attend supplementary programs that will provide them with foundational Jewish identity and competence. Surely, teachers in these schools will need to be retrained to provide a different type of curriculum to accommodate a population of students with a wide range of cultural backgrounds (Russian, Persian, Arabic,

---

an opportunity for initiative and experimentation and it would be tragic to replicate these same mistakes with this new audience.

My model is the bat mitzvah ceremony. It is only in recent years that the bat mitzvah ceremony has become accepted as a cause for public celebration among young women. Yet in far too many cases we simply replicate the same lavish, extravagant and often meaningless parties for young girls that were once held only for young boys. If, as I fear, we will teach young women to study Talmud in the same flawed manner that has yielded only mixed success among young men, we will have learned nothing from the bat mitzvah and we will be committing a profound educational disservice to boot.

[3] Interestingly, in the sub-group of Israeli-born respondents, those who attended Israeli *mamlakhti* (public non-religious) schools did not consider that experience as exposure to Jewish education.

Eastern European, Latino, etc.) and for whom English is not a native language.

Teacher recruitment and training

Alongside these important demographic trends that have clear impact on the future of our schools and communities, there are equally significant considerations that influence the professionals who will staff our schools and educational programs. For one example, it is very difficult to communicate to educators-in-training, particularly to young men with intensive yeshiva learning, the substantial need for teachers in early childhood programs, younger elementary grades and even in middle school. When considering their career aspirations, most male students in our graduate school, for example, want to mainly deliver high-level Talmudic discourses in major programs of advanced Jewish learning, regardless of the large number of contenders for those limited positions and the greater demand for day school pedagogues.[4]

By the same token, there is a growing number of young Jewish families seeking a clean, wholesome, safe environment to place their two or three year-old children, families who would otherwise never consider Jewish education for their children. This represents a narrow window of opportunity by which we may draw them into the circle of Jewish values and community. A good early childhood program with components of family education may convince them to affiliate with other Jewish institutions and continue into the early school years and beyond.

Here we have a prime avenue to reach some one-third of American-born adults and half of the immigrant adult population who have had no exposure to any form of Jewish educational experience, as noted earlier.[5] Sadly, early childhood education has not been a front-burner issue among American Jews and is only now emerging as an institutional and communal concern. Our interest in recruitment and reten-

---

4 Ed.– See also Zvi Grumet, "Transitions in the Life of an Educator", *Ten Daat* Vol. X:1, Adar 5757, Spring 1997, viewable online at http://www.daat.ac.il/daat/english/ten-daat/grumet-1.htm

5 Ed. – See also Mark Rosen, "Beginning at the Beginning: What Should the Jewish Community be Doing for New Jewish Parents?" in this volume.

tion must include this as well. I often wonder about an entire generation of our children whose earliest and fondest memories are Jamaican lullabies and Polish fairy tales.

Issues of training, recruitment and retention affect all sectors of the American Jewish community, albeit in different ways. Anecdotal evidence suggests that in the non-day school world (e.g., congregational, supplementary and Hebrew schools) there is at least the culture and the language of professional excellence. At the same time, however, the level of Jewish literacy (including familiarity with tradition, rituals, practices, and textual knowledge) for these same teachers is woefully inadequate, and a significant portion of early childhood teachers are not even Jewish.

Day schools, on the other hand, seem to be faced with the reverse. Their graduates, both male and female continue in a variety of institutions of higher Jewish learning both in Israel and the US. They compile a wealth of advanced knowledge and crave to share that knowledge at its highest levels. A closer look, however, too often reveals that they really seek self-fulfillment by finding a framework in which to continue their own Jewish learning. For family, social, economic and other reasons, the only acceptable modality available for many of them to continue their studies is to be in a teaching environment.

Their primary motivation is personal and this affects their professionalism, for they simply do not define themselves first and foremost as educators. Moreover, this often impacts significantly on the types of educational environments they seek. Only half-joking, I sometimes counsel young men that if their primary motivation is to continue their Jewish learning, they would be better served by entering another profession, dentistry perhaps, with fixed hours. That would permit them to earn a comfortable living and still have time for their own Jewish study.

By contrast, I warn them that to be an effective educator requires substantial professional preparation to deal with the variety of issues which arise: to "teach Torah" is important, but one also must "teach children." That means developing new skills and learning from models of excellence in the world of education alongside those from their religious and academic circles.

We have, on the one hand, a marvelous pool of young people with an enormous potential, and on the other hand, significant needs in the community and its educational institutions. There are new opportunities for teachers to touch populations that are untouched and to fill the gaps in our loosely structured educational system. It is critical that we bring the appropriate kinds of professional development to both the day school and non-day school worlds, so as to maximize the educational potential for the changing Jewish community of the future.

Assessing Emerging Identity among Religious High School Students: Reflections on the Israeli experience[1]

Yisrael Rich

This presentation discusses a project I have been associated with for several years in which a questionnaire – the *Dyokan* (Portrait) – was developed for the purpose of assessing emerging identity among Jewish adolescents attending religious high schools. Our experience in this area involves students attending Israeli public religious schools but I believe that there are also important implications of the research program for educators in Jewish religious schools in North America and elsewhere.

I first offer four comments to provide necessary background to understand the intellectual and socio-political underpinnings that have shaped this project. The contents of these comments are not closely related, if at all; they merely reflect ideas that have significantly influenced this effort to assess adolescent emergent identity. The first two comments relate to the nature of religious education in Israel.

Over the last 15 years, numerous religious and community leaders and lay persons have expressed a great deal of concern about what they perceive as an inadequate level of religious observance among many graduates of the public religious education system. This issue has been widely discussed and debated in the Israeli mass media, in professional and scientific conferences, in academic and popular publications and at virtually every forum where modern Orthodox Jewish families gather.[2] It is noteworthy that research has demonstrated relatively little erosion of religious belief or practice when considering the entire student body served by Israeli public religious schools from

[1] I especially thank Dr. Elli Schachter of the School of Education at Bar-Ilan University for his leading contribution to this project. Thanks are also due to the Department for Religious Education at the Israeli Ministry of Education and its director, Shimon Adler, and to the Office of the Chief Scientist of the Ministry for their support of this research.

[2] See Sheleg, Y., *ha-Datiyim ha-Ḥadashim*, (Jerusalem: Keter, 2000).

1990 to 1999.[3] However, this fact has had little effect on assuaging the anxieties of upper middle-class families where increasing numbers of male teenagers attending yeshiva high schools have indeed distanced themselves from religious practice. Thus, the concern expressed has been real and relates to events perceived as being close to home.

One should also be aware that an important change in emphasis has been evolving in public religious education in Israel in recent years. The present chief educational officer of public religious education, Shimon Adler, established as a cornerstone of his educational policy to shift emphasis in schools from being "purveyors of knowledge" to "shapers of student identity." Development of personal identity and character has received the highest official priority. In addition, he has mandated educational policy and provided financial support to encourage schools to adopt pedagogical approaches that transform religious studies from analysis of texts construed by many students as irrelevant and archaic into "living Torah," in which Torah learning serves as a practical guide to living all aspects of one's life from the mundane to the sublime.[4]

There are also two broad educational topics unrelated to Israeli religious education that have had considerable influence on this project. The first is the increasing importance of the standards movement that has permeated educational policy and practice in many countries, including the US and Israel.[5] According to this approach, educators must establish clear educational goals for student achievements and should assess regularly and dispassionately whether progress towards these goals meets expectations of various stakeholders. Proponents of this position believe that accountability for achieving goals for students is part and parcel of good educational policy. Although support

---

3 Leslau, A. and Rich, Y., "Seker Talmidei Kitot Yud-bet ba-Ḥinukh ha-Mamlakhti-Dati – 5759," Research report, Bar-Ilan University, The Institute for the Study and Promotion of Religious Education (2001).

4 Adler, S., "Teḥushat Goral O Teḥushat Yiud," *Ḥozer ha-Minhal ha-Dati* 1(2003): 5-13

5 E.g., Darling-Hammond, L., "Standards, accountability, and school reform," *Teachers College Record* 106(2004): 1047-1065; Stringfield, S., & Yakimowski-Srebnick, M., "Promises, progress, problems, and paradoxes of three phases of accountability: A longitudinal case study of the Baltimore City Public Schools," *American Educational Research Journal* 42(2005): 43-75.

for standards-based education is rather recent in the US, it is noteworthy that the *bagrut* matriculation exams in Israel have for many years served as powerful standards that affect what is learned and how the curriculum is presented. Additional national assessment devices have been added to Israeli education in the last decade (e.g., *meitzav*), further strengthening the tendency to monitor educational outcomes according to national criteria.

Finally, development of the *Dyokan* was inspired by research over the last 25 years which has demonstrated that meaningful, comprehensive school-wide change will be executed and institutionalized most effectively when the entire school is the treatment unit. Educational change experts have learned to talk less about teachers or principals or students in need of treatment and to talk more about school norms and culture and how they interact with people who play central roles in the school setting.[6] Many professionals involved in school change now endorse the premise that efforts to improve how a school functions have a reasonable chance of accomplishing the goals of the change effort if the school is viewed as a single unit with interdependent parts. However, when the change program alters the behavior or beliefs of a particular component of a complex social institution such as a school we likely will have only superficial, short-lived effects of the change.

In brief, important influences on this project included:

a) the concern felt by the public religious educational establishment in Israel about inculcating in its students a sincere identification with religious belief and practice;

b) the desire of the heads of public religious schooling to encourage school principals and other educators to think seriously about developing student identity;

c) endorsement of the idea that educational goals must be established and progress towards achieving those goals must be monitored regularly;

d) intellectual support for the strategy that directs efforts to accomplish comprehensive educational change towards the entire school rather than to a particular school segment.

---

6 Sarason, S., *The culture of the school and the problem of change* (Boston: Allyn and Bacon, 1982).

With these issues shaping the *zeitgeist* of religious education in Israel, Shimon Adler turned to researchers at the Stern Institute for the Study and Advancement of Religious Education at Bar-Ilan University to construct an instrument that can aid schools to assess how well they are functioning regarding the development of their students' identity. Note that I did not say "Jewish identity." Rather, the mandate we received was to relate to student identity in a broad manner in which the individual's religious identity is a meaningful component but not necessarily the primary one.

After extensive consultations Adler established three primary goals for this project:

1) To highlight developing student identity as a legitimate and even central goal of public religious education

2) To develop an effective tool for internal assessment at the school level that provides information on the quality of school functioning regarding enhancing student identity

3) To enable policy makers at the national level to analyze the functioning of broad groups of schools or students (e.g. comprehensive school students, female students, etc.).

The task of the Stern Institute team was to accomplish the latter two goals.

Examining Identity

Let us now step back from the central concern of this project to examine the notion of identity, first regarding its meaning as a broad psychological concept and following that we will discuss its relevance to Israeli religious education. This analysis will also touch upon some elements of the rationale for the components of the identity assessment instrument.[7]

Erik Erikson is the spiritual and intellectual father of the concept of identity, describing it identity as "an invigorating sense of sameness and continuity."[8] An individual who has attained identity senses that

---

[7] For a more comprehensive discussion of these issues see Schachter, S., Rich, Y., & Rubin, O., Report on Development of the Dyokan: Stage II, Report submitted to the Office of the Chief Scientist of the Ministry of Education and Culture (School of Education, Bar-Ilan University, Ramat Gan, Israel, in press) (Hebrew).

[8] Erikson, E., *Identity: Youth and crisis* (New York: Norton, 1968).

he or she is the same person from place to place, from time to time. Despite variation in what one does, with whom, and the circumstances of the action, there is continuity in how an individual lives his or her life. What is truly of value remains valuable regardless of place or time or others' opinions. Life has a certain continuity and consistency and it has meaningful content. One can use the term "ego-strength" to characterize persons who have attained identity. Erikson posited that the main developmental task of adolescence is to develop and crystallize a meaningful sense of identity so as the individual moves on to adulthood he or she can state clearly "who I am." This enables the person to live an autonomous, satisfying life according to his or her standards. The developed sense of identity and autonomy becomes a key to adult mental health and an integrated personality. Without that mature sense of identity, one lacks a core essence and is like a leaf in the breeze changing views and beliefs based on whatever environmental pressures one is exposed to. Erikson suggests that it is the responsibility of adults to provide an atmosphere of security to young people and a variety of identity role models so that they can actively explore different possibilities without fear and determine what is most appropriate for them.

Marcia[9] extended significantly the Eriksonian concept of identity. He spoke of a hierarchy of quality of identity development based on two elements – *exploration* and *commitment.* Exploration refers to the examination of alternative ways of thinking about oneself and one's surroundings as identity takes shape. Under proper circumstances, as time goes on the examination leads to commitment to certain ideas, tentative at first, where one tests the waters and ultimately endorses an idea and becomes committed to it or rejects it and continues the process of exploration.

Marcia described four categories of individuals who have or have not conducted meaningful exploration and who have or have not arrived at commitment.

Identity attainment is the most positive condition that characterizes only that individual who has conducted a fairly thorough exploration and after reflection has arrived at certain commitments.

---

[9] Marcia, J., "Identity in adolescence," In J. Adelson (Ed.), *Handbook of adolescent psychology* (pp. 159-187) (New York: Wiley, 1980).

Moratorium is the next positive situation and is presumed to characterize many adolescents. Here the individual has explored meaningfully (and may still be in the exploration process) but has not yet arrived at full-blown commitments about self.

Following this is *foreclosure*, in which exploration has not taken place but commitment is strong usually based on the transmitted standards of significant others. Obviously the day may come when the individual realizes, often with pain, that he or she is not autonomous but rather leading life according to others' wishes.

Finally, the least positive form of identity is *identity confusion*, marked by little exploration and little commitment, and in which identity has no core strength.

The last two decades have seen a great upsurge in scholarly interest in identity development and some important departures from the Eriksonian model as interpreted by Marcia. Many scholars have come to question Marcia's concept of a unitary qualitative hierarchy of identity types. Some authors have highlighted the multi-dimensional nature of identity development.[10] Others have drawn attention to the importance of interactions between the individual and society in determining identity.[11] Several theorists have incorporated postmodern thinking into identity development challenging very fundamental principles promulgated by Erikson,[12] and still others proposed new developmental stages, re-conceptualizing the period of young adulthood. [13] As we will see shortly these modifications of traditional Eriksonian theory have important implications for educational practice.

---

[10] See Lerner, R., *Concepts and theories of human development* (Mahwah, NJ: Lawrence Erlbaum, 2002); Schachter, E., "Context and identity formation: A theoretical analysis and a case study," *Journal of Adolescent Research* 20(2005): 375-395.

[11] Grotevant, H., "Toward a process model of identity formation," *Journal of Adolescent Research* 2(1987): 203-222.

[12] See Côté, J., "Identity: A multidimensional approach," in G. Adams, R. Montemayor & T. Gullota (Eds.), *Psychosocial development during adolescence* (pp. 130-180) (London: Sage, 1996); Gergen, K., *The saturated self: Dilemmas of identity in contemporary life* (New York: Basic Books 1991).

[13] Arnett, J., *Emerging adulthood* (New York: Oxford University Press, 2004).

Identity development in a religious public school

Identity development is an especially thorny topic for public religious education in Israel, where inherent tensions exist regarding tradition and modernity that affect how individuals and schools might view developing student identity.[14] Educators must reflect on core questions: What elements of Jewish culture should be maintained and what should be renewed? What academic subjects should school emphasize and what character traits should be encouraged? Should educational efforts focus on academic progress or character development? What are the boundaries of participation in secular life? Israeli students in the public religious sector have long been encouraged to participate in all constructive aspects of secular society. This ideology continues to be championed while at the same time the lack of boundaries between aspirations of religious youth and those of secular youth is being called into question. Resolution of these and other issues directly affects educators' explicit and implicit models of "good identity" that they present to students and the kinds of identity-promoting events taking place in school.

Another issue contributing to the complexity of identity development is the large degree of heterogeneity of students attending public religious schools. For example, there are major differences in the religious background and observance of students in the public religious sector. Ever since this educational system came into being many of its students came from families that could be characterized as "traditional" or even "non-observant." Their motivation for attending religious schools ranges from a desire for exposure to traditional Jewish subject matter without intensive religious commitment to preference for schools with a minimum of drugs, bullying and other negative social phenomena. Other students in public religious schooling could be characterized as coming from fervently Orthodox families with nationalistic beliefs (*Ḥardalim*). They attend public rather than private *ḥaredi* schools primarily because the latter discourage strong allegiance to the State of Israel and to its institutions. Public religious schools have also long been characterized by significant socio-economic dif-

[14] See Liebman, C., "The evolvement of neo-traditionalism among Orthodox Jews in Israel," *Megamot* 27(1982): 231-249 (Hebrew); Rosenak, M., *Commandments and concerns: Jewish religious education in secular society* (Philadelphia: Jewish Publication Society, 1987).

ferences between students. Many schools are populated primarily by students who come from relatively poor homes, most of whom are of *Sephardic* origin with a significant percentage of children whose roots are in Ethiopia, while a minority of students is from well-to-do homes. Heterogeneity of the student body is an important factor that complicates issues of personal identity because there is no clear consensus regarding "appropriate" identities of students. Is there a single core identity appropriate for all students that allows for cultural and other variation towards which we should be educating our children?

Identity takes shape in particular educational and ideological cultural contexts. Within modern Orthodox Israeli society this context had not changed radically for 25 years, but this is no longer the case. Until very recently, the proposition of incorporating all sectors of the Land of Israel into the State and settling the areas with Jews was a powerful idea energizing much of the religious-Zionist public, including educational institutions.

But recent events in Gush Katif have shattered this notion and no comparable powerful educational-ideological idea has replaced it. For many students the goals toward which national and religious identity development aspired have changed dramatically and now confusion reigns where relative certainty was a comforting fact of life.

Gender identity and its implications for religious practice and belief and family life has also undergone considerable change in the last 10-15 years. Although for quite a few years most female high school students in the public religious sector expressed a desire to combine family and work as adults,[15] we are now witness to aspirations of young women to combine a family with a full demanding career. Furthermore, many young women have raised their voices in questioning traditional forms of Jewish learning and worship in the Orthodox fold that limit or belittle their roles because they are women.[16] For many senior high school females the educational and ideological context of identity formation and crystallization no longer provides clear guidance.

---

15 Golan, R., & Rich, Y., "Career plans for male-dominated occupations among female seniors in religious and secular high schools," *Adolescence* 27(1992): 73-86.

16 E.g., Ross, T., *Expanding the Palace of Torah: Orthodoxy and feminism* (Lebanon, NH: Brandeis University Press, 2004)

Educational implications

What are the educational implications of these ideas? The scope of this article does not allow for a complete examination, but I will note a few points telegraphically.

First, there is growing recognition that facilitation of students' healthy personal identity is an important concern for educators.[17] Within public religious schools there is consensus that schools are important settings that can and should be designed to provide meaningful contexts for positive adolescent identity development and not only in the religious sphere.

Second, schools should provide teenagers with the skills necessary to explore their world effectively and to reflect on their experiences so that they can make thoughtful commitments if they desire to do so.

Third, schools should also provide young people meaningful opportunities to explore and to make commitments, albeit tentative ones.

Finally, in consideration of the multidimensional nature of identity, schools should expose adolescents to diverse stimuli, especially a variety of desirable adult role models, in a secure non-threatening atmosphere that includes "loose guidance" from educators that encourages questioning and scaffolds support for students as they seek personally meaningful answers.

We should now have a better grasp of the concept of identity and the role schools might play in promoting its development. Yet, we still must try to make sense of the idea of "religious identity" if we are to assess it. To do so we need to confront four questions.

First, is it appropriate to rank different religious identities? Is an identity that celebrates religious experience, for example, better or worse than an identity that emphasizes practice? Should the development of one type of identity be encouraged by schools and the other discouraged? Intuitively we answer "no". Different types of religious identity within the Orthodox fold seem perfectly legitimate, even beneficial for different individuals. So, what identity might be considered a positive state for modern Orthodox young adults?

Second, the heterogeneity we spoke of earlier means that there may well be diverse conceptions of a good Jewish identity among different

---

17 Lannegrand-Willems, L., & Bosma, H., "Identity development-in-context: The school as an important context for identity development," *Identity* 6(2006): 85-113.

constituencies of public religious schooling. Might we be in danger of ranking different Jewish groups' conceptions of Jewish identity? Implicitly might we not declare to some of our students that their brand of Jewish identity is inferior?

Third, traditionally most scientists have measured Jewish religious commitment according to discrete behavioral indicators.[18] The problem here – and with belief indicators as well – is whether it is reasonable to determine that the particular behaviors examined reflect accurately one's religious commitment. Many of us have come to believe that this is a very tenuous position.

Finally, kids in 10th, 11th or even 12th grades are only in the "sixth inning" when it comes to identity development. The process is still ongoing. Nothing has been finalized yet. How do we measure identity development when we do not know for certain what stages one must pass through to arrive at satisfactory identity crystallization?

Confronting these questions led us to opt for a process rather than outcome orientation to the assessment of identity development. Within a "process orientation" school is viewed as a setting where identity development can be nurtured proactively. Especially important is the assumption that certain school-wide processes are critical for facilitating identity development. Thus, assessment of the existence of these processes can give us a reasonably good indication of the quality of schooling for promoting healthy identity. We are aware that adopting a process orientation does not answer the questions raised above regarding the meaning of religious identity – and they do deserve serious consideration. Space limitations prevent us from discussing these issues at length; I will merely highlight several advantages of the process approach. One, it allows educators interested in facilitating identity development to focus on particular elements of school life. One can relate to academic elements, social-emotional components of schooling, or other content areas and ask whether particular

[18] E.g., Ben Meir, Y. and Kedem, P., "Madad Datiyut Avur ha-Ukhlusiyah ha-Yehudit be-Yisrael," *Megamot* 24(1979): 362-353; Leslau, A. and Bar Lev, M., "Olamam ha-Dati Shel Bogrei ha-Ḥinukh ha-Mamlakhti-Dati," Research report, Bar-Ilan University, The Sociological Institutue for the Study of Communities (1993); Rich, Y., & Iluz, S., "Perceptions of the purpose of education among religious teacher education students in Israel," *Religious Education* 98(2004): 180-196.

school processes differentially facilitate student identity development in specific areas of student life. Second, a process orientation allows educators to more easily focus on action and enables a smoother transition from a diagnostic mode to questions of intervention and school improvement. Third, process emphasizes school responsibility to confront problems. If, for example, educators argue that outcomes of schooling cannot be improved significantly due to the poor religious characteristics of the student body, they can be reminded that it is their responsibility to foster school processes that ultimately yield desirable development. According to the process approach to identity development, perhaps in contrast to issues of academic achievement, standards of quality will relate to school processes rather than to student outcomes.

In addition to the principles discussed above that guided us in the construction of the *Dyokan,* several "technical" issues were also of importance. First, the Office of Public Religious Education demanded anonymity of participation for individuals and schools in order to facilitate honest responding and educational treatments based on accurate readings of school life. Second, it was important that the instrument would be easily accessible and usable by school-based educators. Finally, we wanted to produce a psychometrically sound instrument.

Constructing the *Dyokan*

Construction of the *Dyokan* involved a lengthy and complex process that we can only sketch in broad strokes. We interviewed numerous students, teachers, and administrators in public religious schools in order to understand how they think about issues related to identity and schooling. We also read official and semi-official documents in which the educational policy and practices of public religious schools was discussed. Protocols of committee meetings, especially the Torat Ḥayyim committee chaired by Rabbi Yaakov Ariel, were examined carefully to better understand differences of opinion.[19] Finally, we reviewed the professional literature on identity development and

[19] Ministry of Education, Culture and Sport Office of Religious Education. Summary and Recommendations of the Torat Ḥayyim Committee (Rabbi Yaakov Ariel, Chair) (Jerusalem: Ministry of Education, Culture and Sport, 2005)(Hebrew).

schooling. Items for the questionnaire were generated from a variety of sources especially those noted above.

After a series of quantitative and qualitative pretests we arrived at seven scales, each of which comprised four to seven items soliciting students' assessments of their school experiences.

In its first major administration, the *Dyokan* was presented to 11th grade students representing a national sample of public religious high schools. Over 5000 students in 120+ comprehensive, academic, yeshiva and *ulpana*[20] schools took part in the initial cohort. Of special interest is the fact that the *Dyokan* was administered in school via the Internet so that students would feel total anonymity and responses could be coded quickly and efficiently. Data from this analysis were subjected to factor analysis and internal reliability values were estimated. In addition, the relationship between *Dyokan* scores and a series of key demographic and educational variables (e.g., SES, gender, religious self-definition, geographic location) was assessed.

Since assessment of the initial cohort, two additional administrations have taken place. Responding to feedback from school principals who were interested in monitoring the development of intact classes through three years of high school, we broadened the scope of student respondents in the most recent administration and presented the questionnaire to students in all grade levels of the high school. All together, over 10,000 adolescents from 150+ schools have completed the *Dyokan* since inception.

Feedback from principals and teachers and statistical analyses led us to make a number of changes in the scales and items of the questionnaire. At the present stage of development the *Dyokan* includes eight school climate scales (40 items) which assess, from the student's perspective, a variety of school phenomena relevant to processes that presumably contribute to positive identity formation in religious schools. Following appear the names of the scales, number of items per scale, alpha internal reliability values, brief descriptions of the scale meaning and sample items:

1. *Prominence of Identity Issues in School* (6 items; α=0.85). This scale measures whether students feel identity issues are addressed prominently in their school. Item examples include:

---

[20] An *ulpana* is the women's equivalent of a yeshiva high school.

- "Many teachers deal with important real-life issues in class and they aren't satisfied just with teaching 'pure' academics."
- "School does a lot to foster students' spiritual, social and emotional growth."

2. *Personal, Available and Caring Teacher*s (4 items; α=0.86). Teachers are perceived as adults who deeply care about their students, relate to them in a personal manner and are available to them when needed. Some examples of items:

- "I get the feeling that teachers care about me as a person."
- "Teachers give you the feeling that they are approachable."

3. *Teachers as Role Models* (5 items; α=0.85). Significant numbers of teachers represent a variety of kinds of individuals that students can emulate and strive to be like when they get older. Teachers are religious, moral and embody virtues that facilitate student identity and academic development. Item examples include:

- "Some of the school staff are people with whom I identify and respect."
- "I would be pleased to adopt many of my teachers' values."

4. *Order and Positive Discipline* (6 items; α=0.80). Teachers create order in the classroom that enables students to learn well and to explore and develop personally with a sense of security. Some scale items are:

- "Sometimes I feel that our teachers are completely helpless facing students in the classroom."
- "In my school there is a reasonable amount of order and discipline and we can learn."

5. *Meaningful Academic Curriculum* (6 items; α=0.84). General academic studies are relevant and meaningful to the lives of students. For example:

- "The studies in my school are a waste of time – they're boring and unimportant."
- "Over the years I've learned in school quite a lot that was important and meaningful."

6. *Meaningful Jewish Studies Curriculum* (4 items; α=0.86). Jewish studies are relevant and meaningful to students. Two examples follow:

- "I feel that much of my time spent in religious studies is pointless and unimportant."
- "The way religious studies are taught here increases my appetite for more learning."

7. *Student Voice & Empowerment* (4 items; α=0.84). Students' ideas and opinions really count and school staff members listen to them.

- "Decisions in this school are made by the administration and teachers only but students aren't ever consulted."
- "We get the feeling in school that the opinions of students are important."

8. *Non-Alienating Religious Climate* (5 items; α=0.76). The religious atmosphere in the school allows each student to explore and to express him/herself without fear of recrimination. Examples of items include:

- "The school encourages students to find their own religious path without pressuring them."
- "If a student expresses doubts about some religious issue some teachers will get nervous, uptight, angry or critical."

If the majority of students at the appropriate grade level complete the questionnaire, the school principal, and only the principal, will receive results of each scale in tabular and graphic form for each class, grade level and for the entire school. These scores can be compared to national norms or to more specific school groups (e.g., yeshiva high schools; low SES schools etc.) according to the principal's request. A representative of the *Dyokan* staff contacts the school principal shortly after receiving the results and offers assistance in understanding the results and in organizing the staff toward school improvement deliberations. Until recently only limited resources were made available by the Department of Religious Education to support schools in planning and executing school treatment programs. Following discussions with Ministry officials it appears that more substantial resources will become available in the coming school year.

We can make no claims for revolutionary improvement in how public religious schools function following assessment using the *Dyokan.* Furthermore, there remain several problems associated with the administration of the *Dyokan,* such as frustrating computer glitches and the perception of repetitiveness. Yet it does seem, after just more than two years of work with the *Dyokan,* that there is far greater awareness among educators of the role of schools in enhancing identity development. Furthermore, feedback from principals based on a survey we conducted leads us to estimate that approximately 25% of the schools that administered the questionnaire embarked on an ambitious school improvement program in the area of identity development. An additional 33-50% of the schools conducted serious discussions regarding *Dyokan* results and instituted some changes. Clearly the *Dyokan* is beginning to have an impact on religious education in Israel.

Although this program has been designed for Israeli public religious education, there is little doubt that many of the concerns that originally inspired this project are relevant to Jewish schools in North America and elsewhere in the Western world.

Issues of enhancing student identity and concerns about authentic and meaningful religious experiences for young people are characteristic of discussions of Jewish education wherever there are Jewish schools. Furthermore, some of the issues making student identity development so complex in Israeli public religious schools, such as heterogeneity of the student body, are equally problematic when dealing with Jewish schools outside of Israel.

On the other hand, there are important differences between public religious education in Israel and Jewish religious and community schools in North America. We note briefly three such differences. First, Jewish schools in North America are usually private and require parents and community institutions to make an especially onerous financial commitment. Thus, compared to the Israeli situation many parents feel a greater sense of involvement in school life and the right to influence school policy. Second, being members of a diverse minority group with deep roots in the local community, Jewish adolescents in North America may have to cope with a somewhat different set of identity challenges compared to their Israeli counterparts. Third, North American Jewish schools are often more autonomous than Israeli schools and are only loosely connected to a central educational agency. Thus, religious and educational policy is shaped to a large degree by local concerns and can exhibit greater flexibility.

Despite these and other differences I sense that many Jewish educators in North America share the desire to establish student identity development as a primary purpose of secondary education. Accordingly, we encourage educators and researchers of Jewish education to consider building upon our experiences with the *Dyokan*. An effort of this nature would endeavor to formally situate student identity development as a central purpose of Jewish education and would seek suitable strategies and tools to monitor how well this purpose is being accomplished. In this postmodern era that presents unique challenges and opportunities to all segments of the Jewish people, facilitation of student identity clarification and growth appears to be an increasingly important purpose of Jewish education.

Does Israel Really Matter?
Knowledge and attitudes of Jewish-American students in Israeli post high school yeshiva/ seminary programs

Irwin J. Mansdorf

In two sequential surveys, the knowledge and attitudes of post high school yeshiva/seminary students from the United States studying in Israel were analyzed. Questions focused on general knowledge of the Arab-Israeli conflict as well as modern Zionist/Israel history. Results showed major gaps in knowledge in the group. Attitudes towards general Israel advocacy were also mixed. A follow up survey seemed to indicate that these students view their Israel experience as one that is primarily devoted to religious development. There are indications, however, that many students would welcome the opportunity to be better versed in Israel studies.

Introduction

The post high school "year in Israel" has become a rite of passage for many, if not most, graduates of Orthodox Jewish day schools in the United States. These programs typically involve a year or two of intensive religious studies, following which students return to the United States to begin college studies.

In the United States, the issue of activism on behalf of Israel has received considerable attention of late. Several organizations have been involved in bringing speakers to campuses while others have focused on training and education. An umbrella organization, the *Israel Campus Coalition*, was formed in 2002 to foster and promote Israel education and advocacy on campuses throughout the country.

The fact that such a large cadre of future college students is present in Israel for an extended period of time presents a unique opportunity to prepare them for the challenge of confronting anti-Israel activity in the United States. In theory, these students, given their strong Jewish education and level of religious observance, have a base of knowledge and level of Jewish commitment which would make them excellent candidates for leadership on the campuses they would attend. Moreover, these students represent what is probably the "elite" of Jewish education in the United States, attending day schools for most of their educational years.

During the 2003-2004 academic year, and under an initiative of the office of Minister Natan Sharansky, a group of volunteers and volunteer organizations met to discuss the possibilities of working with these students to develop a program that would prepare them to take part in pro-Israel advocacy in the United States. While anecdotal reports indicated that these students often have reasons for studying in Israel that are not necessarily related to Zionism or Israel-related activism, it was still thought that knowledge of Israel would be relatively high, as would motivation for learning more. In the absence of any empirical data concerning either the basic knowledge level of the students regarding the "hot button" issues of the conflict or their attitudes regarding pro-Israel activism, preparation for such a project would be incomplete.

To help develop this program, a survey of basic knowledge and attitudes was conducted among a random sample of the yeshiva/seminary students.

The initial survey

The survey instrument consisted of two parts. The first was a 25-question quiz, in multiple-choice format, with 4 choices per question. The second part was an 8-item attitude screen, using a 7-point Likert scale that ranged from "not at all" to "very much".

For the "knowledge" part of the survey, questions reviewed areas related to modern Israeli and Zionist history, civil society in Israel, and issues central to the conflict and current political events in the country. Questions were designed to assess knowledge of basic issues related to settlements, the "occupation", UN resolutions and other arguments presented by pro-Palestinian Arab advocates. Among the four choices for answers, one was clearly correct while the others were, for the most part, totally unrelated to the question. For individuals familiar with the issues, the choices should have not posed great difficulty. The attitude survey attempted to ascertain motivation on the part of the students to participate in pro-Israel advocacy while in Israel and upon their return to the United States. The survey was designed to take no more than 20 minutes to complete.

The participants

Participants comprised a "convenience sample" of both male and female students studying in Jerusalem area institutions. While this presents a less than ideal sampling, administrative issues impeded collection of data in a more stratified fashion.

All participants were volunteers, and all information was anonymous. While about 100 students completed the survey, many more were approached but declined, citing either lack of desire or a concern (after quickly looking at the survey instrument) that they would not be able to answer questions correctly. Most administrations of the instrument were proctored, and in small groups. In several additional unproctored administrations, a pattern of questionable responses was noted, putting into doubt and subsequently invalidating many other protocols. The data ultimately reported is of the proctored protocols only.

Students appeared to represent a cross-section of those studying in Israel, coming from five separate institutions in the proctored group and many more in the unproctored sample.

Another group of approximately 50 students completed a modified, fill-in version of the instrument. In this administration, answers were left up to the students for many of the questions. Data from this group are also not reported, although a review of the some of the answers will be discussed.

Serving as a control group was a group of American students currently attending universities in the US who had volunteered to participate in a 2-week course in Israel on pro-Israel advocacy. Questions for the control group were identical for Part A, but two items in Part B (relating to study in Israel and religious attitudes) were not relevant for the group and thus omitted.

Administration of the instrument for the control group took place following completion of their course in January 2004. Administration for the yeshiva/seminary students took place over a two-month period from mid-January through mid-March 2004.[1]

---

[1] Appendix I provides sample questions from the survey instrument as well as results.

Results

The expectation was that students with the more intense educational and religious background would have a comprehensive knowledge of Israel, similar to expectations about their knowledge of other Jewish issues. It was further hypothesized that a year of intensive study in Israel would strengthen this knowledge, and be reflected in a desire to learn and be involved more on Israel-related and Zionist inspired activities.

The results of the survey appear to indicate major gaps in knowledge among the yeshiva/seminary student population. Motivation for pro-Israel activism also appears to be modicum, with attitude responses falling in the middle range of the Likert scale.

For the yeshiva/seminary group, there were few questions which were answered correctly by more than 60-70% of the students, and many questions were answered correctly by only 25-35% of the respondents, a level of proficiency which could be expected by random choice of answers. Approximately 65% were able to correctly define "Zionism," and less than half had familiarity with issues such as refugees, the partition of Palestine, the British mandate, the Oslo agreements or the Geneva Accords. Only 44% recognized that the Golan Heights is being demanded by Syria or that Yamit was part of territory returned by Israel to Egypt. Half the students were unable to identify Menaḥem Begin as being associated with the bombing of the King David Hotel.

Among the control group, results were considerably different. For the most part, these students did not have the extensive formal Jewish schooling which characterized the yeshiva/seminary group. Despite the background gap, in the knowledge component of the survey their scores were consistently higher than the yeshiva/seminary group, with gaps ranging from 5-45% per question.

Differences were also evident in the attitudinal section of the survey. Attitudes among the yeshiva/seminary group were characterized by moderate responses; the only response showing "moderately high" ratings was the question on the importance of being involved in pro-Israel advocacy. Even on this item, the motivation or willingness to participate in training was "moderate" at best. More telling was the fact that the group only attached moderate importance to learning about the Arab-Israel conflict during the year they are spending in Israel.

The control group showed answers that were at least "moderately high" on all items, demonstrating not only a recognition that pro-Israel advocacy is important, but also a willingness and motivation to put this into action by personal example. This is not surprising, since this group was a self-selected sample of activists who volunteered to further their education in this area.

Analysis of the protocols of the yeshiva/seminary students in which multiple-choice questions were replaced by fill-in questions yielded interesting results. For example, several students identified the "King of Egypt" in response to a question asking them to name an Arab leader that made peace with Israel. In response to a question asking what the Palestine Mandate referred to, students wrote, "The complete destruction of Israel" and "The Jewish state of Israel". A question asking who was responsible for the bombing of the King David Hotel had several students filling in different versions of the phrase "Arab bastards". Many questions were left blank.

All students had the option of adding comments to their protocols. Few in either group took advantage of this option, although comments among those that did in the control group were characterized by a desire for more Israel-related courses and appreciation for the opportunity to participate in the training. The yeshiva/seminary comments were generally less positive in this respect.

Discussion

Questions may be raised as to why the yeshiva/seminary students showed relatively low levels of both knowledge and motivation. From anecdotal reports, it appears that many of these students and the programs they attend place minimal emphasis on learning or improving Hebrew or having social contact with Israelis or Israeli society. Studies focus mostly on religious subjects, with few schools setting time aside for regular classes on Israel or Zionism. The students' movement around Israel is often restricted (either by the schools or by parental mandate), further cutting them off from many of the experiences of mainstream Israel. They appear to have minimal exposure to current events in Israel and often spend extended periods during their year in Israel out of the country, such as during the Passover holiday break, when many students appear to choose being back in the US over experiencing Passover and Yom ha-Shoah in Israel.

All this raises questions as to the nature of any Zionist identity that these students may have. While one cannot dispute the "love of Israel" that many seem to profess, the centrality of Israel as a major nationalistic (as opposed to religious) motif in their lives is considerably less than we would have anticipated. Although non-participation in a survey is not a valid statistical gauge, the anecdotal evidence of students fearing that they would not fair well as a reason for their non-participation strengthens the conclusions drawn from the statistical analysis.

In terms of pro-Israel activism of US college students, this population would certainly appear to have the "credentials" to be natural leaders. What appears to be needed, however, is an educational component that would provide these students with the facts of the conflict and the knowledge with which to effectively combat anti-Israel attitudes. If the attitude survey results are accurate, however, many students do not view this as something they would personally involve themselves in, thus placing in question the practical significance of any such training.

Because the sample was a "convenience sample" and not necessarily a representative sample, there is the possibility that the data may not reflect the complete reality. Some results suggest that the secondary school attended plays a significant role, and that students from high schools that were associated with a more liberal religious philosophy also appeared to fare better. Many students choosing to attend secular colleges appeared to have at least as much knowledge, if not more, than students choosing to attend Yeshiva or Stern College. Among the control students, most did not attend Jewish day schools, raising questions as to what factors may account for their higher levels of motivation. Methodological issues related to the survey certainly impact on some of the possible interpretations. The results do, however, match many of the anecdotal reports heard from Israelis with American day school backgrounds, including those who have regular contact with the yeshiva/seminary students. A more in-depth and more stringently controlled study is needed to assess the validity of these anecdotal reports.

While few students appear to be "activist" types or possess the desire to be so, this may reflect what is common in the broader Jewish population in the United States. What is of particular note here, however, is that this population is one that has received in-depth Jewish education and religious training, something that sets them apart from the population in general. Contrary to the expectations, the intensive religious instruction does not necessarily translate into Israel-related commitment or knowledge. It appears that there is a cadre of students in the yeshiva/seminary population that has both the knowledge and the motivation to serve as activists on campus, although it is considerably smaller than anticipated. This sub-group would likely self-select in any program that would be available and continue in their activism after their return to the United States.

This study has a number of practical implications. The initiative to recruit and train college activists from this population may be best served if targeted to specific individuals rather than the population as a whole. American day schools may want to conduct their own studies of the matter and test the knowledge and attitudes their students have regarding Israel – and adjust their own programs accordingly. Similarly, yeshiva/seminary programs in Israel may want to re-evaluate their own programs in light of these findings.

These results also have implications for the many initiatives and pro-Israel campus activities that have taken place across campuses in the United States. While some of the programs are well-funded and involve considerable skill on the part of the educators and activists involved, one may ask if there is any solid evidence that there has been any change in the knowledge, behavior or attitudes of students that these efforts are designed to influence. Data on participation in pro-Israel activities are not readily available. Neither are data available that measure attitudes of Jewish students on campus and their knowledge of Israel and issues related to the conflict. Until such data are gathered, the effectiveness of any pro-Israel advocacy training effort remains an open question.

Follow-up survey

A follow-up survey focusing exclusively on attitudes toward Israel study was conducted on a similar sample of yeshiva/seminary students in October 2004. Those students were attending a Shabbaton entitled "The challenge of being a Zionist on campus", sponsored by the Ministry of Jerusalem and Diaspora Affairs and organized by Yavneh Olami. Yavneh Olami, responding to anecdotal reports that there is a need to address Israel/Zionist education in this population, has taken upon itself the goal of promoting those values.

A total of 28 out of a group of about 90 students (over 30%) completed the survey that was distributed in the course of the Shabbaton. It is not clear why only some students completed the survey and others did not. Of the 28, 15 identified themselves as male and 5 as female. The other 8 students who completed the survey did not identify their gender.

It is likely that this group of students voluntarily attending the Shabbaton represented a self-selected group that had a higher degree of interest in pro-Israeli activism than one would normally find among the general yeshiva/seminary population. These students, including those that completed the survey, did so following two days of intensive exposure to a variety of Zionism-related topics, including an address by Minister Natan Sharansky. Results should be evaluated with this fact in mind. In this sense, they share some important characteristics of the control group in the initial study.

The survey format

The present survey was in dual response "forced choice" format. "Forced choice" surveys have both advantages and disadvantages. On the minus side, the limited choices available and the lack of fill-in or essay items force the respondent to make what may not be a choice that truly reflects attitude. Moreover, when the scale is limited to only two items, both of which may be true to varying degrees, the choice of one over the other may be difficult and not reflective of the relative degree of applicability of each individual item. On the other hand, limited "forced choice" also has a critical advantage when it comes to examining and determining narrow and specific attitudes, as in the present survey. The structure of such scales forces respondents to carefully weigh specific options and make a choice as to which option is the stronger preference. When properly administered, it allows for both respondents and researchers to "select sides" and determine the most appropriate or relevant choice among choices presented.

That was the goal in the present survey. Considering the variety of possible reasons, feelings and opinions that these students have regarding their study in Israel, an attempt was made to clearly focus on some specific choices, as reflected in the specific survey items. Following a series of informal discussions with individual students studying in Israel, and in light of comments received following the earlier survey, a 10-item "forced choice" type attitude survey was constructed. Some of the items in the survey were quite direct in their focus on the "year-in-Israel", while others were more generally related to overall Jewish issues of concern. The items were not presented in any particular order.

The survey was voluntarily completed without any supervision or administration. Not all the students properly completed each item, accounting for the difference in total responses per item. Only properly completed responses were included in the final tabulations.

Results

The first two items in the study clearly indicate that these students view themselves as religiously observant and see the world, including Israel, through those eyes. In overwhelming fashion, the students responded that the major goal of their year is to solidify their religious identify and deepen their Torah knowledge. While experiencing Israeli culture may be a subordinate goal, it is clearly not the major reason they came to Israel. They also view improving their spoken Hebrew as less important than furthering their Torah knowledge.

It is difficult to ascertain whether the students actually feel this way, or if these two responses reflect a socially ordered attitude that is popular in this population. In any case, the strong response pattern here demonstrates that successfully teaching pro-Israel activism or Zionism to this group needs to include at least the perception that it is taking place within a religious framework. Informal evidence suggests that most "year" programs for these students do not provide any formal training or education in Zionism, Israeli culture, politics or history.

The religious worldview of these students is reflected in another response pattern. By a margin of almost 4-1, they indicated that they considered assimilation a greater threat than anti-Semitism. Consistent with that viewpoint, less than half the respondents felt that Holocaust studies need to be stressed more than study of *Navi*.

Despite this "religio-centered" orientation, students overwhelmingly indicated that they would find a pro-Palestinian rally on their campus more troubling than a Reform service being conducted in the campus synagogue. At first glance this would appear to be inconsistent with other answers on the survey, especially the item where students noted that assimilation was a greater threat than global anti-Semitism. One would think that these students would view Reform services as an example of assimilation and a Palestinian student rally as an example of global anti-Semitism, but this was clearly not the case. One possible explanation for the shift is the presentation of the issue as personal rather than communal. Another possibility is that the students viewed the question as one which would require a level of "political correctness". It also may be that, as opposed to the more abstract question regarding anti-Semitism and assimilation, when the questions are personal and concrete, practical considerations play a more significant role.

Some of the patterns in other items were inconclusive, but appeared to indicate limited interest in what could be described as functional activities related to identifying with Israel. For example, the group was split evenly between their choice of attending a Blue Fringe (a popular band featuring Orthodox students who recently spent a year in an Israeli yeshiva) concert or a lecture by Shimon Peres, as they were with regard to spending a *Shana Bet* year in a *Sherut Leumi* type program rather than a yeshiva/seminary. It would be interesting to see what the actual response would be if such programs and activities were in fact available to students.

Some of the responses offered may be nothing more than an age-appropriate social pattern for the students surveyed. It may be that with some more maturity, and in another physical venue (such as a campus), the activities chosen would be different.

Discussion

While this survey suffers from certain methodological issues, such as random selection of respondents and internal validity of the items used, it is another piece of evidence that corroborates anecdotal reports on the behavior and attitudes of the population surveyed. As such, it offers further insight into the issue of "year-in-Israel" students.

The focus of this survey was exclusively in the realm of attitudes related to studying in Israel and students' overall worldview, as distinct from the initial survey in which knowledge of Israeli culture, politics or history was measured. In general, it appeared that these students, even after 12 years of intensive Jewish education, contend that their post high school year in Israel is primarily to strengthen their religious identity and to further religious studies. Insofar as these goals require a major time commitment and leave little if any time for any other pursuits, the fact that these studies physically take place in Israel can be said to be incidental and largely irrelevant. One could argue that the same religious goals could be reached with a similar oriented program anywhere in the world.

While they are in Israel for their studies, these students adopt a mantle of religiosity that needs to be considered, so that the teaching of Zionism and Israel-related matters would appear to best take place in a religious environment for these students. Ideally, one-year programs would formally incorporate courses on Israel, Hebrew language, Israeli politics, civics and history in an effort to provide practical tools for students on their return to campuses in the United States. Such courses, if made mandatory, would also serve to fill in a much needed gap in knowledge that these students lack so long as day schools and high schools in the United States continue to lag in providing this knowledge base. In practice, however, few yeshiva/seminary programs offer such coursework or are prepared with appropriate faculty to offer it. Programs such as those offered by Yavneh Olami are held for students who choose to attend in their free time and are conducted only in some school settings.

One other open question is the religiosity of lecturers in such programs. In planning one such program with an American Orthodox group, one of the American educators stipulated that the lecturers need to be "people who would be acceptable to our type of student", leaving no doubt that what was meant was that the lecturers would also need to be Orthodox. Whether the students themselves would agree with such a demand is not clear, since they all have had non-religious (and even non-Jewish) teachers in the past and will certainly have them in the future. The insinuation appears to have been that when it comes to Israel, the only view these students should be exposed to is one that is framed through religious eyes. The relevance of this type of approach to the subject of Israel-related activism on campus is certainly questionable. What is clear, however, is that there is a great deal of pressure among this group to appear, act and think in a specifically prescribed fashion.

It should be noted that these surveys were completed on-site immediately after an intensive Shabbaton that included almost non-stop lectures for two days on topics related to Israel and Zionism. Despite this, students saw the goals of experiencing Israeli culture and improving Hebrew as secondary to their primary purpose in Israel, i.e., strengthening religious identity. From the responses to the last question in the survey, it would appear that even these students recognize that their Zionist education leaves much to be desired. Just as important, however, is that the present sample is probably not representative of the general "year-in-Israel" student population in that these students actually voluntarily chose to attend an Israel-activism related seminar. It would not be unreasonable to conclude that the present group was unique insofar as most typical "year-in-Israel" students would likely show far less interest in the topics presented.

Retrospective anecdotal reports from the Shabbaton seem to bear out some of the assumptions made regarding the background the students brought with them to Israel. Lecturers reported having to improvise and modify presentations because of the clear lack of knowledge that the students demonstrated. In a "Show what you know" session, most students could not identify photographs of Rav Kook and David Ben-Gurion, and most had never heard of Aḥad Ha-am. The exception was a few knowledgeable students and some "Write on for Israel" graduates.[2]

The results also point out what may be a distinct difference between these students and other types of American students in Israel. It is probably safe to say that for students who attend Israeli universities, or special programs sponsored by groups such as Young Judea or Camp Ramah, the choice to be in Israel is driven primarily by a desire to undergo a distinctly Israeli experience. As such, they may be more

2 "Write On for Israel" http://www.writeonforisrael.org/ is an advocacy journalism project for high-school students sponsored by *The Jewish Week* (NY).

receptive to topics and programs that involve pro-Israeli activism and Israeli history and culture. In the case of the typical yeshiva/seminary student, however, the motivation to be in Israel is apparently driven by other factors. While these factors include the religious element seen here, they are likely to include other factors such as social and/or peer pressures as well.

Currently, the major focus in the yeshiva/seminary programs still stresses the "year of Jewish learning" more than the "year in Israel". Hopefully, educators will begin to see that learning about Israel, its people, history, culture, politics and challenges should be a major a goal for American Orthodox students in and of itself. Until such time, however, we can expect student knowledge of and attitudes toward the Zionist enterprise to be sub-optimal, with the attendant implications for their lives on college campuses and beyond.

Appendix I

Sample questions and responses from the instrument used in the initial survey.

	% of correct responses in	
	control group	yeshiva/ seminary group
1) "Zionism" is a concept that is best defined as: a. Membership in pro-Israel organizations b. The national liberation movement of the Jewish people c. A movement that fights anti-Semitism d. The rights of Israel to the West Bank and Gaza	88	66
2) Arabs in Israel: a. Cannot become full citizens b. Are encouraged to emigrate c. Are all Moslems d. Have full rights as any other Israeli	93	54
4) The right of Jews to a homeland was affirmed by: a. The Balfour Declaration in 1917 b. The European Community in 1948 c. The Versailles Conference in 1919 d. The Yalta Conference in 1945	98	71
5) Which one of the following fought for Israel in 1948? a. Yitzchak Rabin b. Bibi Netanyahu c. Natan Sharansky d. Ehud Barak	79	50

	% of correct responses in	
	control group	yeshiva/ seminary group
10) The "Palestine Mandate" refers to: a. The Turkish rule in the area b. The Arab desire for a state c. The British rule in the area d. The United Nations partition resolution	81	30
12) Who was responsible for the bombing of the King David Hotel? a. Yasser Arafat b. Menachem Begin c. Osama Bin Laden d. Gamel Abdul Nassar	81	50
13) Which one of the following Arab leaders made peace with Israel? a. Anwar Sadat b. Hosni Mubarak c. Abu Mazen d. Saeb Erekat	98	61
14) The charter of the PLO calls for: a. Peaceful co-existence with Israel b. Israel to honor UN resolutions c. Armed struggle to liberate the land d. Cooperation with Hamas by the Arabs	95	53

	% of correct responses in control group	yeshiva/ seminary group
16) The "Law of Return" refers to: a. Persecuted Jews obtaining Israeli citizenship while abroad b. The Arab demand for refugees to return to Israel c. Any Jew's right to obtain Israeli citizenship d. Arab laws demanding that Israel return land to the Palestinians	74	59
17) Which of the following areas were returned by Israel to Egypt? a. Alexandria b. Ramallah c. Gaza d. Yamit	84	44
21) Palestinians claim international law is against Israeli settlements because of: a. The 4th Geneva Convention b. The Red Sea Summit agreement c. The UN commission on human rights d. The Hague international court	74	29
23) The Golan Heights: a. Is being demanded by the Palestinians as part of their homeland b. Was always Israeli territory c. Is being demanded by Syria d. Was captured from Lebanon	86	45

	% of correct responses in	
	control group	yeshiva/ seminary group
24) The "Road Map" refers to: a. A peace plan proposed by Arik Sharon b. A proposal promoted by the United States c. A plan to combat anti-Semitism d. An Arab plan for resolving the conflict	91	64

Appendix II

Questions and responses from the follow-up survey. These questions each offered two possible responses; numbers in parentheses are numbers of respondents identified with that response.

1) The major goal of the "year in Israel" should be:
a. solidifying one's religious identity (22)
b. experiencing Israeli culture (1)

2) Which of the following is a more important goal for the "year in Israel"?
a. Improving spoken Hebrew skills (3)
b. Deepening Torah knowledge (22)

3) Which of the following is a bigger threat?
a. Global anti-Semitism (5)
b. Jewish cultural assimilation (19)

4) Which of the following is not stressed enough in Jewish education?
a. Study of the Holocaust (11)
b. Study of *Navi* (13)

5) Which of the following would bother you more?
a. Palestinian student rally near your college campus (26)
b. Reform Sabbath services in your college's synagogue (1)

6) Which of the following would you rather attend?
a. Blue Fringe concert (10)
b. Lecture by Shimon Peres (10)

7) Which of the following would you rather attend?
a. *Pesach Seder* at an Israeli army base (16)
b. *Pesach Seder* with family in the USA (10)

8) Which of the following would you more likely enroll in?
a. *Shana Bet* volunteer program with underprivileged youth in Israel (12)
b. *Shana Bet* additional studies in Yeshiva/seminary (13)

9) Which of the following would you rather go to in your free time?
a. Meeting your visiting high school teacher (11)
b. Attending an IDF induction ceremony (15)

10) Which of the following is a more pressing issue for American Judaism?
a. The problems facing young religious Jewish singles (7)
b. The quality of Zionist education in American Day Schools (20)

Jewish Education in the Postmodern World

Elliot Malamet

Discussing what he sees as the core mandate of current Jewish pedagogy, Moshe Greenberg (Professor Emeritus of Bible at Hebrew University) writes of "the learner as a creature impelled by curiosity concerning the world around him and his own inner life..."[1] When a particular culture is capable of providing its members with appropriate spiritual satisfaction, it will also persist over time.

Schools and their entourages – administrators, teachers, boards, parents, federations – wrestle endlessly with the magic formulae that will satisfy all constituents and provide the children with that most slippery of accomplishments, "a good Jewish education." Greenberg alludes to the fact that in the discussion over what to teach and how to teach it, the principal focus must always be the spiritual potential of each child. To those who argue that the goal of a Jewish school should be to empower children to master classical texts, or to make them conversant with the richness of Jewish history and culture, or to become fluent in the Hebrew language, or to become habituated to Jewish practices, I respectfully demur. Ultimately, all of the above are surely important components of a well rounded student, but the first goal of our contemporary efforts in any Jewish classroom must be inspiration on the existential level and an anticipation of those most central of student questions:

Why should I care? What does Judaism mean to me? How can I make it my own? In what way does it speak to my situation, my aspirations, hopes, anxieties, feelings, fears and frustrations?

I teach at a Jewish community high school spanning grades nine through twelve, which services students of various denominational backgrounds, from unaffiliated to Orthodox. The students' attitudes to Judaism are, of course, impossible to categorize in a few brief brush strokes, but one might be on safe ground in asserting that, more often

---

[1] Moshe Greenberg, in *Visions of Jewish Education*, Seymour Fox, Israel Scheffler and Daniel Marom, eds. (Cambridge University Press, 2003).

than not, on a good day they appreciate Judaism rather than embrace it; on a bad day, they question or simply dismiss its relevance to their current lives. Phrases like "Jewish identity" resound far more on the lips of my students and the parent body than a preoccupation with adhering to *mitzvot* or a desire for intensive involvement with Jewish texts. My students breathe the Internet, watch less TV than people think, and want to belong to something, somewhere.

But less and less is that thing Judaism, a religion they paradoxically know and of which they are often surprisingly ignorant, and to which they attach sentimental value as opposed to fear of the Lord. Judaism is, after all, an "ism" – an ideology of ancient absolutes in an age of moral autonomy. It is my job, each day, to talk about the Old Words – God, Holiness, Tradition, Commandments, Responsibility, Sacrifice, Community, Sin, Soul. It is also my job to speak of the New Words – Spirituality, Pleasure, Self-esteem. Can a religion be loved if it is imposed? Conversely, will it be embraced if it is optional? This paradox has a Zen flavor – the more you squeeze it, the more it vanishes – but its poignancy is felt by parents of all faiths trying to pass on some of their essential religious beliefs and practices.

In Peter Berger's fine book *The Heretical Imperative*,[2] he argues convincingly that modernity involves a shift from fate to choice, from a life almost predestined by the narrowness of options, due to limited technology and mobility and a deeply ingrained code of cultural and religious mores, to a life where almost anything is available and any lifestyle is there for the taking. You can be what you want to be – but do you know what you want to be? Indeed, it often seems that my students' real religion is listening to music; everywhere I look the kids "wanna rock."

What to do? Just give them the information and hope for the best? Teach them the skills that could possibly lead to further learning after high school, teaching them, proverbially, "to fish"? More and more I am persuaded that one important method of negotiating the tug of war between the mantra of independence and the claim of Torah tradition lies in the teacher's ability to present a model – in his or her own real life struggle – of faith and doubt, of fidelity and anguished perplexity. At a time when teaching Judaism must increasingly com-

[2] Peter L. Berger, *The Heretical Imperative* (New York, 1979).

pete with the pull of Western culture's panoply of entertainments and distractions, it becomes incumbent on the teacher to, as it were, step out from "behind" the text and, in selected instances, disclose to the student what the teacher's own life experience can reveal about the complexity of Torah. Michael Rosenak has alluded to the way in which children learn to understand Judaism through the prism of their teacher's experience. He notes, "we must let [the children] in on the discernments that we of the adult community see as the basis of our commitments, yet on their own level."[3]

Self disclosure as an educational tool

How can self-disclosure help to break classroom deadlock? What price is paid for such self-disclosures? How can especially aggressive challenges from students actually work to further the teacher's educational goals? I would like to relate a particular instance of how I grappled with these issues in the course of teaching a famous passage in the Talmud (Yoma 35B) which depicts Hillel, poverty-stricken and unable one day to pay the fee to enter the study hall. After a guard blocks his access, Hillel climbs the roof and remains there "in order to hear the words of the Living God." It is Friday night and snow is steadily falling. He is finally discovered at daybreak by one of the Sages. He is nearly frozen to death.

Much of my students' focus centered on the legitimacy of Hillel's conduct. What possessed Hillel to climb up onto the roof and endanger his life? Though some appreciated Hillel's doggedness, they also perceived him as foolhardy. What of the guard's seemingly uncharitable behavior? Furthermore, what kind of rabbis were these that didn't even know that the guard was running this "bribery scheme"? Are such people to be admired? Far from seeing the story as an admirable example of devotion to Torah study, a traditional approach suggested by many commentaries, for students it constituted a paradigm of religious obliviousness and insularity.

One harmlessly belligerent but popular student asserted that the whole story was "nuts" and that Hillel was just plain "stupid" for going up on the roof.

"I'm sorry, but I think it's totally ridiculous."

---

[3] Michael Rosenak, *Roads to the Palace* (Oxford: Bergahn Books, 1995), p.61.

Classroom freezes momentarily.

Much of Talmudic learning is grounded in a fundamental respect for Jewish figures in general, and *Ḥazal* as a whole. What happens when those boundaries are broken, when the sage is judged as we would anyone else, when the assessment of behavior is taken case by case and aligned with the student's own convictions and sensibilities about rationality, truth, and wrong-headedness? This is obviously but one piece of the larger dilemma in contemporary Jewish education, as the *weltanschauüng* of the student may be radically out of sync with traditional notions of the importance, and perhaps even holiness, of Jewish texts.[4]

We had reached an impasse; any explanation or insight I could offer would only to serve to further remove the Torah from the world of rational discussion. It was as if they were saying, "Okay, we get it. This is Judaism once again exiting from the realm of common sense to hop aboard the train of pious fantasy. Sorry, I'll disembark from that train right now."

I have experienced this moment literally a thousand times in a classroom, whether studying a *halakhic* or *aggadic* passage, a section of *Ḥumash* or a law connected to Shabbat. And while it can be disheartening it can also be inspiring, as it generates an opportunity to try and clarify for myself, and hence for my students, where the deeper possibilities of Talmudic understanding lie. It is precisely at that moment when self-disclosure may be a far more effective facilitator than any amount of textual analysis or citation of commentary.

The risks of self-disclosure

Sharing with my students something I had never shared with either students or colleagues at my school, I told them that I could relate to Hillel's experience as I had once been a folk musician. I remembered the difficulty in getting club owners to let me audition, and how desperately I wanted to play music. And how on one freezing February afternoon I had literally waited all day outside a club, which was closed, to catch a club owner on his way into the club because I didn't

---

[4] Ed. note – For a parallel discussion about Biblical figures see Jacob J. Schacter's "On the Morality of the Patriarchs: Must biblical heroes be perfect?" in this volume.

want to miss him, so that I could play my music. I was, in a sense, up on the roof all day.

Instead of admiration for Hillel's devotion to Torah, my students' predictable inquiries were about what instrument I played, did I sing and, inevitably, could I play for them! Though the stasis had definitely been broken, was the cost a regression in terms of real learning? Gemara cannot easily be made "relevant," and it may be an error to invest in such an enterprise. One of the standard clichés of postmodern literary criticism is that all textual observations are filtered through one's own individual, and hardly unbiased, perspective. Self-disclosure can become a parody of this phenomenon, in the sense of allowing any insight to serve as a legitimate lens on the text, and thus running the enormous risk of trivializing Judaism.

Despite my foreboding, in subsequent class discussions several themes did emerge from the students' comments. Directed away from a literalist obsession with the exact circumstances of Hillel's story and onto the metaphorical possibilities induced by my account, my students began to reflect upon the meaning of sacrifice. For what would they be willing to renounce personal abundance and even their lifestyle? For music, family, love, sex, money, status? For Hillel it was a very plain choice – for "the words of a living God," of a divine message that could transform his life.

The next day, when I returned to studying the text, an unexpected opportunity presented itself. A student asked me whether I'd always been "religious". This question had never presented itself before, and I suspect it reared its head now because I'd given them a whiff of my life "back in the day" and they did not perceive folk clubs and Orthodoxy in the same universe. I admitted that I had only become observant in college and that, although I would be far too afraid to stay up on a roof on a freezing night, I totally related to Hillel's desperate need to be inspired by the spiritual – that, ironically, I saw "the roof" as life saving.

"Why?" asked a student.

"What do you want out of life?" I asked. "When, in a few years, a romantic partner looks you in the eye, what will you draw on to respond? What fills up your inner life? What exists beyond the moment? Who are 'the guards,' so to speak, who block you from the spiritual empowerment that each human being must have in order to really live?" My students were silent but they were listening, and not just in a voyeuristic way. Now we were really talking about that Gemara, really getting down (or up) to Hillel's perch and the life decisions that precede that kind of "ascent."

Does popularizing Torah cheapen it?

Afterwards, however, the reaction of one colleague presented a sobering coda to my experiment. Does the Gemara really become respectable after the teacher shares something of his life? I was highly sympathetic to his plea, reminded as I was of the "paradox" that had so impressed my students (that I could love both Gemara and rock & roll) and enhanced the Talmud in their eyes. For my colleague this was a dubious compliment.

I was led to reconsider the question of what had been accomplished. Had I truly influenced my students to seriously engage with Jewish texts, to inhabit the mindset of those such as Hillel who would willingly give up so much for just a taste of Torah? Or had I simply provided a diversionary distraction, producing a classroom management sleight of hand that pulled the class out of its doldrums in an entirely ephemeral way? The long term answers remain to be seen.

Nervous about the potentially dry core of essential Jewish texts (much of the Talmud, for instance, seems less than kinetic when compared with say, Plato's *Republic*, not to mention the self-help fare lining the shelves of local bookstores), Jewish institutions increasingly have taken to linking their product with popular sounding slogans.

As Erica Brown notes, "This motivation has inspired high gloss brochures and promises of good refreshments after class. One adult education program took an acronym that made it sound like an aerobics class."[5] She observes that many Torah study classes are paired up in a pseudo-trendy manner – "Zen and *Ḥasidut*," or "Gestalt theory and *Sefer Shemot*." While there may be nothing inherently wrong with broadening the scope of Judaism to show its universality, there is a danger when the underlying message seems to be: "Torah can be hip, too – as engaging as Seinfeld, as spiritually healing as Eastern meditation."

[5] Erica Brown, "Jewish Adult Education: Creating an Educational Democracy", *Ten Daat* (9:1), 1990, pp. 63-77.

The teacher – textual enabler or personal mentor?

The concept of disclosure ultimately opens onto the larger issue of the teacher's personality or self. Jewish education contains many proponents of what one might call "formalism" – the text and its commentaries are everything; the teacher is merely a conduit to that end and must keep his own life utterly out of the classroom discussion. The attempt to keep the teacher's personality on the sideline and to "focus on the text" has been a matter of some controversy in academic circles, Jewish and otherwise. To some extent this mirrors the ancient Greek penchant for viewing self-disclosure with suspicion. As one writer puts it, "the Classical Greeks seem to feel that there is something wrong with the autobiographical mode of discourse: only desperate need can redeem it." It would seem that, given the plethora of continuity statistics that have frightened Jewish communities, Jewish education has arrived at an era of desperate need.

Adolescence brings with it the paradoxical thrust to break free of limits together with the desperate hunger for secure boundaries, for a map of existence that can be trusted and enriching. The desire for substance, for what the poet Wallace Stevens so eloquently called the "weight of primary noon, the ABC of being," is alive in many young people yearning for selfhood and a meaning. The teacher thus becomes a key resource for helping the student with that quest.

In this regard, there are central questions that need to be asked in educational research. Who are our teachers? Where do they come from? What is their vision of reality? What can they give of their lives that will show students that Judaism is worth learning and pursuing? Are they willing to take risks emotionally and intellectually to bring Jewish students of this generation to a new relationship with the Word?

The classical debates, of whether textual skills or relevance of content should be central, need to be re-examined in light of the central role of the personhood and personality of the teacher. In the age of choice, where the assumptions of student fidelity to the tradition are no longer a given, teaching Jewish studies needs to be a revelation by teacher to student of the impact that Judaism has made on the teacher's life, and what Torah evokes for the teacher intellectually, emotionally, spiritually. When students turn their gaze to the teacher, they need to see not a mirror of their own lives, but a window into a life beyond that which they know. They want to see that their guides not only appreciate their struggles, but may even have undergone them themselves, learning ways of transcending. And they wish to share in that transcendence.

Beginning at the Beginning: What should the Jewish community be doing for new Jewish parents?

Marc Rosen

Introduction[1]

Data from the National Jewish Population Survey continue to show that more Jewish families are becoming less connected to the Jewish community.[2] Jewish education is one of the best ways to ensure Jewish continuity, but a major unanswered question is whether parents who do not start out connected to the community will choose to educate their children Jewishly.

While this situation is cause for concern, it also presents the community with an opportunity. If the Jewish community reaches out to young Jewish couples when they have a child, there is potentially a 3-5 year window for influencing their future educational choices and the Jewish identity of their children.

To gain a better understanding of Jewish parents and to reach out to them effectively, it is necessary to seek answers to several key questions:

- How is the current generation of new Jewish parents planning to raise their children?
- How do they feel about Judaism and the Jewish community?
- What is the community currently doing for them?

This paper describes research conducted in 2004 by the Cohen Center for Modern Jewish Studies at Brandeis University to answer

---

[1] This research was supported by the Jewish Life Network/Steinhardt Foundation as part of the planning process for the Newborn Gift program. The author wishes to thank Naomi Bar-Yam and Lucy Lorin for their assistance.

[2] Kotler-Berkowitz, L., Cohen, S.M., Ament, J., Klaff, V., Mott F. & Peckerman-Neuman, D. (2003). *The National Jewish Population Study 2000-01: Strength, Challenge and Diversity in the American Jewish Population*. New York: United Jewish Communities.

these questions. It concludes with recommendations for the Jewish community arising from the research findings.

Description of the Research

Focus Groups

To learn about parents' attitudes toward Judaism and their educational plans for their children, a total of 11 focus groups were conducted in five cities: Atlanta, Boston, Chicago, New York, and Seattle. Approximately one hundred parents participated. Participants consisted of non-Orthodox couples and single parents, both in-married and inter-married, who were expecting or who had at least one child age 0-3. Focus groups were organized and hosted by couples in each community who agreed to hold the groups in their homes and recruit their friends and acquaintances. Emphasis was placed on recruiting those who were not strongly connected to the community. The vast majority of participants had had at least some Jewish education while growing up, but only about a third were currently members of a synagogue.

Phone Surveys

To learn about community-based programs for new Jewish parents, several hundred Jewish communal professionals in more than 50 North American communities with a Jewish population of 20,000 or greater were contacted by telephone. Calls were made to the four major agencies in each community most likely to sponsor programs for new parents: Federations, Jewish Community Centers, Jewish Family Services, and Jewish Boards of Education. Although it was impractical to contact every synagogue in each community, calls were made to specific congregations when relevant programs were identified. Interviews were also conducted with some of the regional offices of the Reform, Conservative, and Ḥabad movements to learn about programming conducted under their auspices.

Summary: Focus Group Findings Regarding Parents

Child-Raising

Almost all of the in-married parents expressed pride in being Jewish and wanted their children to have a Jewish identity, but most acknowledged that they did not know how to foster that within their children. Most of these parents did not practice Judaism in their home and did not have sufficient knowledge to teach their children about the tradition. Parents were mixed about whether they were planning to provide their children with a formal Jewish education. Their inclination appeared to be related to their own positive or negative experiences with Jewish education growing up. Many of the intermarried parents had not yet decided on the religion in which their child would be raised.

Connections to the Community

Most parents were receptive to the idea of being contacted by their local Jewish community and wanted to be connected. However, they had not yet made an effort to connect or had not found a suitable place. Synagogues were generally viewed as being too expensive and parents did not feel comfortable coming to services with very young children. Parents were receptive to adult Jewish education, especially when it was targeted for their particular needs and childcare was made available.

The Influence of Peers

Peers were found to be especially influential, since:

- parents want to connect socially with other parents
- parents seek help with parenting from their peers
- peers can provide a non-threatening introduction to Judaism and the Jewish community
- parents are more likely to attend Jewish events with a friend than alone
- peers influence the choice of a preschool

Preschool Choice

Preschool represents parents' first opportunity to make a Jewish educational choice. Parents based their choice of a preschool primarily on school quality and location. Most parents were unwilling to consider a preschool unless it had a good reputation and was less than a 15 minute drive from home. Parents often relied on recommendations from friends when choosing a preschool. Jewish sponsorship, while appreciated, was a secondary consideration, as was cost. In several communities, parents expressed a great deal of concern about the availability of preschool openings and were worried that their child would not be able to get into preschools that were in high demand.

Summary: Phone Survey of Community-Based Programs for New Jewish Parents[3]

Overview

Jewish agencies and organizations in communities across North America have developed an assortment of offerings for new Jewish parents. Program titles, content, format, and sponsors vary widely. Most of the programs generally fall into one of four categories:

- Prenatal education programs
- Shalom Baby gift basket programs
- Developmental and parenting education programs
- JCC parenting centers

Programs are primarily social in their orientation. They give parents a chance to meet, connect, share experiences, form play groups and carpools, or find a good pediatrician. When needs assessments are conducted both formally and informally, institutions report that first and foremost families are looking for ways to connect with other Jewish families.

Prenatal Education Programs

There are three programs of this type run in multiple communities for expectant parents. The challenge faced by all three programs is finding a large enough group of parents who are expecting at the same time.

---

[3] For a more comprehensive description of community programs, see Rosen, M.I., Lorin, L. and Bar-Yam, N. (2004). *Raising Jewish Babies: Community-Based Programs for New Jewish Parents.* Waltham, Massachusetts: Cohen Center for Modern Jewish Studies (www.cmjs.org).

- *LaMazel Tov* is a six-session program offered primarily in the West that is held in synagogues, hospitals, and through *Shalom Baby* programs. In these courses, a rabbi or Jewish educator teaches about Jewish ritual and traditions surrounding childbirth, and a certified childbirth educator or nurse provides medical information.
- *In the Beginning* is a regional, synagogue-based program in Northern California consisting of a "train the trainer" program for individuals who will run *Baby is a Blessing,* a three-session course for expectant couples.
- *Jewish Baby University* is a six-session program offered in Denver and Phoenix that is jointly taught by a rabbi and a childbirth educator. The program includes six hours of Judaic instruction and also covers such practical matters as techniques for pain management, medical interventions, hospital procedures, birthing options, care of the newborn, breast and bottle feeding, and selecting a pediatrician.

Shalom Baby Gift Basket Programs

Approximately 25 communities conduct programs that provide a gift basket to new Jewish parents when they have a baby. Gift baskets are usually funded and distributed by the local Federation or Jewish Community Center under the name *Shalom Baby*, although *Shalom Baby* programs are not necessarily limited to gift baskets and often include other programming. Program directors are usually Federation or Jewish Community Center (JCC) employees. Baskets range in value from $75-100 and are always free to the recipients.

Baskets are sent to both affiliated and unaffiliated Jews. Generally, expectant parents, relatives, or synagogues notify coordinators of a new birth and request a basket. Most gift basket programs have websites with information about how to arrange for a basket. A few communities conduct extensive publicity and advertise the program at synagogues, doctors' offices, kosher establishments, Jewish organizations, and in both local Jewish and secular newspapers.

Doctors and hospitals are viewed as being in the best position to publicize the program to those who are not in contact with the Jewish community. Some *Shalom Baby* programs have networked with hospital chaplains and visit the new parents there. Communities have mixed success at achieving cooperation from the medical community.

Baskets generally include: information on local Jewish resources; information related to the baby's developmental issues; a gift such as a bib, bag, or Jewish board book; and information on Jewish rituals and/or parenting. Most baskets include coupons donated by local Jewish organizations. These offer discounts on Jewish preschool or daycare, JCC membership, or an adult education class. Some program directors solicit additional donations enabling the community to include ritual objects like candlesticks, grape juice, or Jewish prayer books. Baskets may also include books on Jewish parenting and information about local day schools.

Most of the work is done by volunteers who help solicit donations for the baskets, put the baskets together, and deliver them. Volunteers sometimes go beyond just delivering the basket and spend time with the new parents at home. In several communities, home visit programs by trained volunteers extend for a considerable length of time. These visits prove critical when mothers are new to the area and have little or no support system. Some communities view the initial contact as a way of engaging parents in additional programming and volunteers take an active role in connecting mothers to local rabbis and resources.

Overall, the majority of programs reach only a small percentage of the Jewish parents in the community. Programs are most successful when there are home visits by trained volunteers, when the medical community is involved, and when there is follow-up.

Developmental and Parenting Education Programs

Many *Shalom Baby* programs offer educational classes for parents once they have received a gift basket. Other classes are offered without an initial gift basket, such as those sponsored by Jewish Family Services. Topics and titles vary widely – programs have such descriptive titles as *Mother Matters, Miracles and Mayhem: The Realities of Motherhood, Baby Safe, Boot Camp for Jewish Dads, Arts and Tots,* and *Bagels, Blocks, and Beyond.* Programming is generally a mixture of classes and events with Jewish content, and classes addressing the parents' or baby's developmental needs. Classes vary considerably with respect to Jewish content – some have little or none while others have a strong

Jewish orientation. The degree of Jewish content depends upon the receptivity of the target audience, the backgrounds of those teaching the program, the sponsoring agency, and the funding available.

Some programs start out being similar to the educational programs described above, but include children and evolve into playgroups. Such programs are generally sponsored by Jewish Community Centers or Jewish Family Services. Once the formal sessions end, parents often arrange amongst themselves to continue to meet as a playgroup. These groups can continue for years.

JCC Parenting Centers

Parenting centers are physical facilities with appropriately designed space and a resource library. They are located in JCCs and often work in partnership with Jewish Family Services. Needs assessments indicate that mothers often feel isolated at home and need to go somewhere to get out of the house. Parenting centers offer mothers a destination where they can drop in anytime to meet other mothers, get emotional support, and attend educational programs, playgroups, and discussion groups. Books and information on community resources are also available. Memberships are affordable and can be purchased independently of JCC membership. Parenting centers appear to be an especially successful model and are growing rapidly in JCCs across the country. Facilities range from one room to a much larger space.

Success Factors

Although virtually all communities offer at least one of the programs described above, rarely do communities have a set of coordinated programs across agencies. Only a few communities have a community-wide vision. More typically, individual agencies offer programs to fulfill their specific mission, and a single agency takes the lead in a particular community. Which agency this turns out to be differs depending upon the nature of the Jewish organizations in the community. Communities with the most successful programming have the following common features:

- A community-wide vision
- Passionate community leadership
- Inter-agency cooperation
- A strong, highly involved JCC

- Early childhood expertise
- Designated funding

Recommendations for Communities

Find the Parents

A priority for every community is to identify and contact all Jewish couples who are having a baby, especially those who are not presently connected to the community. The research data indicates that many couples are receptive to these contacts and welcome them. Currently, there are only about five communities making a concerted effort to do this through well-designed gift basket programs with trained volunteers. Other communities with gift basket programs do not engage in the same degree of effort to find Jewish couples.

The medical community is an especially effective way to reach parents. Everyone goes to an obstetrician and pediatrician, and a great deal of time is spent waiting in doctors' reception rooms. The community should engage in efforts to cultivate relationships with medical professionals in order to publicize such programs to couples who would not otherwise be reached.

Connect Parents with Peers

Since peers are perhaps the most significant influence on parents' choices, communities should create more opportunities for Jewish parents to meet and socialize with other Jewish parents who are already connected to the community. Parents with leadership potential should be identified and receive training. Parents who are not currently connected to the community are much more likely to become receptive to adult Jewish education and Jewish education for their children if their friends are Jewish and involved with the Jewish community.

Use Financial Resources Strategically

There are three areas that would benefit from additional funding:

- Funds should be allocated to provide tuition subsidies for Jewish preschool
- Funds should be allocated for synagogue memberships and synagogue childcare
- Funds should be allocated to strengthen and support JCC parenting centers

Utilize the Internet

Almost all parents use the Internet to communicate and obtain information. The Internet can be utilized to connect local parents with each other and to provide information about programs, local resources, and Jewish tradition.

Create a National Office

Currently, there is no central address for new parent programs. A national office could:

- Serve as a resource
- Foster communication and coordination across communities
- Identify, learn from, and replicate the best programs around the country
- Offer conferences, training, and newsletters for Jewish communal professionals
- Generate funding

Seize the Opportunity

There are approximately 60,000 Jewish births in the United States annually, but relatively few are being welcomed by the Jewish community. No one in the community appears to be taking responsibility for this group, and this stage of the Jewish life cycle has been largely ignored. Even though there are a number of effective, inexpensive programs for this group, they are not widely known nor are they widely used. These parents are often interested in providing a Jewish identity for their children, but cannot do so themselves and are not reaching out to the community. It is incumbent upon the community to reach out to these parents, since such efforts have a great deal of potential to influence the Jewish identities and education of the next generation.

Afterword
Jewish Education: It's time to rock the boat

Aryeh Rubin

More than a billion dollars has been spent in the last ten years to stem the tide of assimilation, but most would agree that significant progress has yet to be made. What is crystal clear to me is that the educators hold the key to that progress. Statistics don't lie. The 2001 Population Study shows that the assimilation rate for Jews who attended day school is 7%, while the national average is 47%. Day school enrollment, particularly among the Orthodox, continues to grow, and there are now twice as many students enrolled as forty years ago.

Yet, as important as Jewish education is to our survival and mission, more and more families are struggling to keep up with tuition costs, despite the fact that American Jews earn on average twice the median American income. Teachers are overworked, under-paid, less appreciated than they should be, and the likelihood is that they will not have their own children enter the field of Jewish education.

Conferences like this need to do more than stimulate – they need to spark a *mahapekha* – a revolution. They need to provoke the educators to muster *ḥutzpah* – to approach, if not demand from the funding organizations that they up the ante.

As a people, our leadership has too often failed us in its passivity: during the Holocaust, with the crisis of assimilation, and with the Israeli/Palestinian public relations debacle. We cannot allow the education of our Jewish children to meet a similar fate.

We should learn from the success of the Soviet Jewry movement. The establishment in the early 1960s universally insisted on a "quiet diplomacy." The World Jewish Congress, the Rav at Yeshiva University, and even the *Ḥassidic* Rebbes, they all insisted that we *za shtil*, that we keep quiet. In the face of that quiet, one man in 1964, Jacob Birnbaum, organized some college students to start the Student Struggle for Soviet Jewry. Despite opposition, they organized the early rallies, got the momentum going, and it was the simple people – the *amkha* that provoked the establishment to join the bandwagon. Once the establishment signed on, they, in turn organized the marches on Washington, and the rest is history. Soviet Jewry was saved, and it was the beginning of the empowerment of American Jewry. If we are to turn the tide in Jewish education, it will have to come from us, the *amkha*.

Anecdotal evidence shows that a majority of the board members at many Federations do not send their children to day schools. If these schools were of the caliber of, say, Dalton, St. Albans, or Pinecrest, perhaps they would. But as it stands, the quality of our education is clearly not the priority it should be at the funding organizations. True, these umbrella organizations have to feed the hungry, house the homeless, heal the sick, and care for the elderly. But we must reexamine our priorities if we are to have the continuity that we all claim is crucial. More resources must be made available for Jewish education.

The assets are there. According to *Moment Magazine,* some twenty-five billion dollars is sitting in Jewish foundations, yet a recent report indicated that only 11% of major gifts from such organizations goes to Jewish causes. We, they, all of us, are not trying hard enough. The educators, both individually and collectively, have to go to their boards, their local central agencies for Jewish education, and demand more resources, take out ads, and start alternative funding campaigns. Quiet diplomacy will not work – it never has.

This is the time for action. If we do not take action we will not get the resources, and if we do not have the resources the unaffiliated will not be part of the system, and regrettably many will never learn of the grandeur and majesty of our heritage.

We need to be righteously indignant. For as much as we strive to perfect ourselves as individuals, history will judge us not on our ideas or beliefs but on the community and society we have created. That is contingent on our ability to reinvigorate our educational system – and without the cooperation and support of the umbrella funding organizations it will not happen.

We also need to rethink what we expect our children to know, what we should be teaching them, and how we should be teaching them. The stimuli available to a ten-year-old today were unthinkable only fifteen years ago. We have to rethink how we will make learning more effective and how we will introduce technology and its capabilities into our somewhat archaic system of pedagogy.

When all of the extant Jewish literature, from the *Tanakh* to the Yiddish literature of the *Haskalah*, from the *Rishonim* to the Jewish Encyclopedia, can all fit on a single disc and is instantly searchable and accessible, perhaps we need to rethink what learning means. I know that we don't have the answers, but we need to ask the questions.

To accomplish this all we need are two things: the ability to think outside the box, and the funding.

With training and foresight, many educators are willing and do think outside the box. As for money, that is where the educators in the trenches have not been fighting for their share. What we need is for teachers, principals, boards, and parents to unite and light that magical fire to force the hand of the established funding organizations.

Pirke Avot says, "Every dispute that is for a heavenly cause will eventually endure." I, for one, cannot think of a more heavenly cause.

About the Contributors

Scott J. Goldberg is Assistant Professor at Yeshiva University's Azrieli Graduate School of Jewish Education and Administration, where he is also the Director of the Fanya Gottesfeld-Heller Division of Doctoral Studies. He holds a Ph.D. in Applied Psychology from New York University, an M.S.Ed. in Special Education from Bank Street College of Education in New York, and a B.A. in Jewish Studies from the University of Chicago. Dr. Goldberg is an active researcher of various educational and psychological topics including multilingual literacy development and assessment, the connection between learning disabilities and behavior problems, the effects of media on learning and behavior, bilingual education, and special education.

Zvi Grumet is the Associate Educational Director of The Lookstein Center. After two decades as a teacher and administrator in The Frisch School, HAFTR, Hillel (NJ) and Torah Academy of Bergen County, he made Jerusalem his home. He teaches *Tanakh* and Jewish pedagogy at Machon Pardes and directs the *Tanakh* department at Yeshivat Eretz Hatzvi, both in Jerusalem. Rabbi Grumet has published numerous articles both on *Tanakh* and educational topics and is a popular lecturer in Jerusalem and abroad.

Elliott Malamet lectures in the Jewish Studies Department at Queen's University in Kingston, Ontario and head of the Jewish Thought Department at the Community Hebrew Academy of Toronto. He has done extensive work in the field of spiritual education and conducted seminars on teaching Judaism to young people in the United States, Canada, England and Israel. Dr. Malamet is currently at work on a book which examines the ethics of teenagers.

Irwin J. (Yitzchak) Mansdorf is a psychologist living in Israel. He is a founder of MATAN crisis intervention services in Israel and has had considerable experience in developing systems of intervention in dealing with terror and war-related stress. Dr. Mansdorf frequently writes and speaks on issues related to Israel.

David Pelcovitz is professor of education and psychology at Azrieli Graduate School of Jewish Education and Administration. He is a leading expert in family trauma, child abuse, and at-risk youth, particularly as these issues affect the Jewish community. He has conducted education and parenting conferences worldwide and is the author of numerous scholarly articles as well as two popular books, *Balancing Parenting* and *The Parenting Path.* Dr. Pelcovitz's research in trauma counseling includes family members of September 11 terror fatalities, survivors of terrorist attacks in Israel, and tsunami victims in Indonesia.

Yisrael Rich received his Ph.D. in Educational Psychology from the University of Minnesota in 1974 after which he made *aliyah* and joined the School of Education at Bar-Ilan University. His research focus includes teachers' and counselors' educational beliefs, adolescent planning of future work and family roles, and religious education. He has authored or co-edited five books and published numerous articles. Professor Rich served as Director of the Stern Institute for the Study and Advancement of Religious Education and as Chair of the Board of Directors of The Lookstein Center, both at Bar-Ilan University.

Mark I. Rosen is a Senior Research Associate at the Cohen Center for Modern Jewish Studies at Brandeis University. His research activities on the Jewish community have explored such diverse topics as intermarriage, Reform movement outreach, financial incentives for day school parents, Birthright Israel, Jewish life on college campuses, and Jewish summer camping. He has recently completed a case study on Hillel: The Foundation for Jewish Campus Life, and is conducting research on programs developed by the Jewish community to engage Jewish parents with young children. Dr. Rosen is also the author of *Thank You for Being Such a Pain*, a book of *mussar* teachings on difficult relationships.

Aryeh Rubin is the Director of *Targum Shlishi*, a foundation dedicated to providing a range of creative solutions to problems facing Jewry today, with a particular focus on education, women's issues, Israel and justice for Nazi war crimes. Premised on the conviction that dynamic change and adaptation have historically been crucial to a vibrant and relevant Judaism and to the survival of its people, *Targum Shlishi*'s initiatives are designed to stimulate the development of new ideas and innovative strategies that will enable Jewish life, its culture, and its traditions to continue to flourish.

Jacob J. Schacter is University Professor of Jewish History and Thought and Senior Scholar at the Center for the Jewish Future at Yeshiva University. He served as Dean of the Rabbi Joseph B. Soloveitchik Institute in Boston from 2000-2005, and from 1981-2000 was the Rabbi of The Jewish Center in New York City. He was the Founding Editor of *The Torah u-Madda Journal*, and has authored nearly fifty articles and reviews in Hebrew and English. He is also the editor of *Reverence, Righteousness and Rahamanut: Essays in Memory of Rabbi Dr. Leo Jung*, *Jewish Tradition and The Nontraditional Jew*, and *Judaism's Encounter with other Cultures: Rejection or Integration?*, and co-editor of *The Complete Service for the Period of Bereavement.* Rabbi Dr. Schacter recently published *The Lord is Righteous in All His Ways: Reflections on the Tish'ah be-Av Kinot* featuring the teachings of Rabbi Soloveitchik, and is completing a new Hebrew edition of the autobiography of Rabbi Jacob Emden.

David J. Schnall is dean of Yeshiva University's Azrieli Graduate School of Jewish Education and Administration. After serving as professor in the department of public administration at Long Island University for 12 years, he was appointed to the Herbert Schiff Chair in Management and Administration at Yeshiva University's Wurzweiler School of Social Work in 1991. In 1999, Dr. Schnall was awarded a Fulbright Foreign Scholarship. He also served as a U.S. State Department consultant for non-Governmental Organizations for the Government of Cyprus.

Moshe Sokolow is Fanya Gottesfeld-Heller Professor of Jewish Education at the Azrieli Graduate School of Jewish Education and Administration of Yeshiva University. Dr. Sokolow has authored numerous educational guides related to the works of Rabbi Joseph Soloveitchik and Nechama Leibowitz. He is the editor of *Ten Da'at: A Journal of Jewish Education*, and *Texts & Topics: Curricular & Instructional Materials for Jewish Educators.*

Stuart Zweiter is the director of the Lookstein Center for Jewish Education in the Diaspora at Bar-Ilan University, a leading resource center and think tank for Jewish education. In Israel, he has also served as an instructor in Talmud in Bar-Ilan University and as a fellow at the Shalom Hartman Institute. In the U.S., he served as a principal at the Hebrew Academy of the Five Towns and Rockaway High School and at the Frisch School in Paramus, New Jersey. He has served as an educational consultant to communities throughout the world.

About the Lookstein Center

The Rabbi Dr. Joseph H. Lookstein Center for Jewish Education in the Diaspora of the School of Education at Bar-Ilan University is a service and research center deeply committed to enhancing the quality of Jewish education in the Diaspora.

The Center seeks to develop and facilitate programs and projects that reflect, encourage, and foster ongoing growth and learning for the Jewish educator.

The Center's work is driven and inspired by the belief that there is much to be gained by creating frameworks that nurture and support the symbiosis between:

- The rich educational and spiritual resources in Israel and the particular experience of the Diaspora
- Educators from the broad range of the Jewish community
- The world of practice and the world of Jewish and general knowledge

---

Lookstein.org promotes the establishment of a worldwide interactive community of Jewish educators and providing a wealth of easily accessible pedagogic resources. The website includes:

- asynchronous moderated discussion groups which already include over 3000 participants,
- real-time conference rooms presenting lectures on issues in the Jewish day school,
- an archive of ideas and materials contributed by educators,
- educational materials and online lesson-plans developed by Lookstein Center professionals,
- a registry of schools and educators,
- a bulletin board of professional opportunities and events,
- an online helpdesk,
- on-line access to a large selection of curricula and instructional materials.

The Principals' Program facilitates professional development and provides ongoing support and resources for day school educational administrators, and serves as a catalyst for creative strategic planning for

Jewish day schools. The program addresses the multi-faceted world of the Jewish day school from the perspective of school culture, and focuses on action research as a tool for planning and leading educational change. The Principals' Program presents an opportunity, unique in the world today for Jewish educators, to master the leadership challenge of navigating the multi-faceted worlds of the Jewish day school.

The Remote Teacher Programs: Since 2002, The Lookstein Center has been a leader in video conferencing for day schools, both for students and teacher training. With the rapid development of communication systems, making video-conference systems more accessible and easier to use, day schools around the world can now benefit from teachers living in Israel coming into their classroom and teaching their students on a weekly basis.

Jewish Educational Leadership is a professional journal for Jewish educators published by The Lookstein Center. The journal was designed to increase the exposure of Jewish educators to general research and advances in education and focus on the applicability of these findings to the world of Jewish education. The journal also:

- provides a forum for publishing research in Jewish education,
- offers access to new trends and methodologies in Jewish education,
- serves as a center for publicizing innovations in the field,
- brings classic Hebrew texts that focus on education to an English speaking audience.

Curriculum and Professional Development Projects. The Lookstein Center has served and serves in a consulting role in ongoing programs with individual schools or groups of schools in North America, Australia, England, Hong Kong, South America, and the Former Soviet Union in long-term curriculum and staff development projects, school evaluations, and programs of overall school improvement.

Research Projects. The Center engages in academic research which serves to direct and enhance the Center's extensive range of practical program applications.

Printed in the United States
90280LV00004B/377/A

9 780976 986201